Webplicity

Webplicity

The Critical Guide to Successful Web Strategies

Bill Young with Michael Sevilla

iUniverse, Inc.
New York Lincoln Shanghai

Webplicity
The Critical Guide to Successful Web Strategies

Copyright © 2005 by Bill Young

iUniverse books may be ordered through booksellers or by contacting:

iUniverse
2021 Pine Lake Road, Suite 100
Lincoln, NE 68512
www.iuniverse.com
1-800-Authors (1-800-288-4677)

ISBN: 0-595-34575-1

Printed in the United States of America

CONTENTS

XploreNet, Inc. www.xplorenet.com 303.573.1118

ACKNOWLEDGEMENTS

I would like to think the following people for their help and support:

- My wonderful wife Karen for being a great example of humility, love, and strength
- Co founder Treg Meldrum for always going above and beyond
- Michael Sevilla for his incredible intellect and talent
- Mike Jaltuch for being the technology guru so the rest of us don't have to
- Michel Vallee and Gisela Stadelmann for their patience and support
- My sister Sally and parents Pete Young and Penny Asher
- My supportive Grandparents "The Gibbs"
- Karen Runchel for her outstanding editing skills
- Our clients for choosing XploreNet
- All my friends for understanding my obsessive compulsive entrepreneurial disorder

HOW TO USE THIS BOOK

This book sheds some light on the subject of how to build a Web project, be it a Web site or complex Web application. We're sure you've seen the good, the bad, and the ugly when it comes to Web sites and Web applications. The Web is filled with examples of ineffective work, so XploreNet decided it made sense to take our knowledge and process and save the world. Well, maybe not save the world, but at least try to save business executives, owners, and front line marketing and IT personnel from nightmare Web projects.

Developing a new Web project is a tricky process no matter how you go about it. The XploreNet team has been implementing Web-based solutions since 1997 and the process is still a difficult one. This book covers our process, experience, and success in implementing over 500 unique solutions for some of the most successful businesses in the U.S. Furthermore, we reveal some of our *secrets* and present you with many ideas. We won't reveal to you the "secret sauce," that's purely proprietary, but here, in this book, we'll offer you valuable insight that may very well make the difference in your Web project being a success or a failure. The key to getting started on a successful Web project is a well-developed Web plan. What it contains and includes is the hard part.

In this book, we take you through the process of developing a Web plan step by step, and show you how your Web strategies, business goals, and specific projects fit into the plan. Whether you are the CEO, VP/Director of Marketing, CIO, CTO, Director of IT, or a business owner, this book can help you complete your most important business goals. In addition, whether you are a small firm attempting to redesign a basic Web site or a large organization implementing a complex tool, the five modules (if completed properly) will ensure the most complex Web project runs smoothly.

Five modules will help you through the process:

MODULE 1:   Covers the Analysis Phase of the process, showing you how to get started on the right foot.

MODULE 2:   Contains the Blueprint to success. Just as an architect completes blueprint drawings for a dwelling, you must complete both a site and project blueprint in order for your Web project to be successful.

MODULE 3:	Covers the Construction Phase—no need to get your hands dirty or buy work gloves.
MODULE 4:	Discusses the Promotion Phase of any new Web Site or Web based tool.
MODULE 5:	Covers the steps to putting everything together and provides an example of a successful Web plan outline.

The outlined processes in this book are tried and true methods that help facilitate success for any sized firm, on any sized project.

The best way to use this book is to understand the entire Web plan format and use it on your next Web project.

In the end, our hope is that this book helps you put all the pieces of the puzzle together to successfully launch your next generation Web project.

Welcome to a successful Web project.

WEB PLAN OVERVIEW

HOW DO YOU BUILD A WEB SITE OR ONLINE TOOL? At XploreNet we've heard this question countless times. A better question might be how do you build a *successful* Web site?

Why do we get this question so often? The reality is that most firms are stuck in the past when it comes to their Web strategies. There is enough information available on the Internet to fill Wrigley Field five times over. Yet figuring out the best solutions and paths to obtainment can give anyone a headache.

What is a Successful Web Project?

Why do only half of Web projects obtain the definition of a successful project? According to CIO Insight, only 40 percent of CIOs say they have a Web project plan in place. No wonder only two-thirds of projects are likely to come in on budget and less than 60 percent are likely to achieve their ROI targets.

In this book, we're attempting to answer this question by providing a map to help guide your Web project from the **present** to the **future**. Most successful businesses have a business plan and some even have marketing plans, but very few have a real Web plan. In order to reach the ultimate goals for your organization you must have a business plan, marketing plan, and a Web plan.

How?

We'll show you. We cover five modules in this book:

▸▸ Module 1: Analysis

▸▸ Module 2: Blue Print

▸▸ Module 3: Construct

▸▸ Module 4: Drive

▸▸ Module 5: Putting it all together.

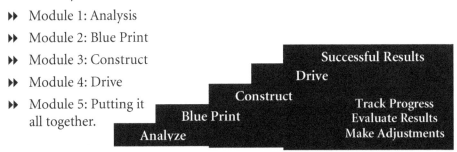

It may seem like a daunting process to complete a detailed plan; however, the success of your new Web project may depend on your fully developed Web plan.

MODULE 1: ANALYSIS

1.0 Analysis

This module discusses the first phase of understanding how your Web project fits into your Web strategies and defines your Web plan. As you read, you will quickly understand whether your Web strategies are on life support or are dead. In today's competitive business environment, companies which successfully implement a new redesign or build a complex Web tool, routinely look back to the initial Analysis Phase as the foundation to their success. A well-defined Web strategy includes an interactive, customer focused, Web presence and "user-friendly" Web applications. If you overlook something in the Analysis Phase, then the rest might be meaningless.

Business Web sites today need a plan in order to remain competitive. Early Web sites served simply as glorified online brochures. Now they must produce something tangible. Of course the site must be visually appealing, but the content must also have a point.

This means: multiple portals for different audiences; secure, encrypted e-commerce sites; secure back-end systems for storing employee, vendor, and customer information; real-time data integration to inventory databases, and customer resource management (CRM) systems; and a simple processes for usability. Issues regarding design and complexity change based on the size and scope of your firm, however, everyone wants an interactive and successful Web project.

The XploreNet Web Plan was developed during the past seven years. It is based on our Intelligent Development System (IDS)™. This plan incorporates a detailed Web strategy that covers how to build the correct Web presence, integrate the proper applications, and promote the site to the right audience,

<u>for maximum results</u>. No matter what a business or organization offers, it must have the right strategies and a professional Web presence in order to be competitive in today's business world. It is critical for profit oriented, traditional corporations, that sell products, to have an outstanding presence, but non-profits and service-providing organizations, such as lawyers and charities, must have a quality Web presence as well.

The Analysis Phase is critical to marketing vice presidents and directors who must understand how each marketing initiative fits into the Web picture. IT managers must also understand how projects will be implemented and business objectives matched. Finally, C-level executives and business owners must understand how the Web site and online marketing strategies fit into the business as a whole, and quantify real business revenue and ROI.

Most books and Web firms cover an Analysis Phase based strictly on data (Web traffic reports, metrics, conversion rates, etc.). In this book, XploreNet covers those important areas, but also delves in-depth, into the business reasons for a Web analysis, providing a case study at the beginning of Modules 1 and 2 to show the Web plan in action.

Understanding your Web strategies and implementing the right solutions is more than just data. It is about matching every part of your Web site, project tools, and Web strategies to your business and marketing objectives.

CASE STUDY

The American Water Works Association Research Foundation, known as AwwaRF, is a member supported, international, non-profit organization, that sponsors research that enables water utilities, public health agencies, and other professionals to provide safe and affordable drinking water to consumers.

Situation: AwwaRF had a productive Web presence, but realized it was time to modernize the Web presence. After looking at 12 different firms they chose XploreNet to help them facilitate collaboration and growth, positioning the Foundation as the world leader in research on water.

Impact: XploreNet put a Web plan together that included an intense Analysis Phase, reviewing AwwaRF's past experience, defining the Web project's purpose and goals, understanding who should be involved, helping to develop the staff, defining success, and establishing ROI,. XploreNet completely restructured the AwwaRF Web site, making large portions of it database-driven, pulling content, not only from a database on the Web site, but also directly from AwwaRF's proprietary database at their central office. The end result is a site, which is not only much easier to navigate but also delivers up-to-the-second, current content. The new site's subscriber feedback has been overwhelmingly positive.

AwwaRF's ability to complete the Analysis Phase proved critical in the successful redesign of their Web presence. View the site at www.awwarf.org.

Past Experience (1.1)

Purpose:	Determine your current situation by understanding what's right and what's wrong

Key Points:	Putting your past experiences to work for you and starting fresh enables your new project to hit the necessary goals head on. Understanding where you've been will help you get to where you need to go. You want to learn from what you did well as well as from what you did wrong.

What was it like the last time you redesigned a Web project? Did it remind you of the last time you went in for a root canal? Many things might have gone wrong the last time around including:

▶▶ Long exhaustive meetings that produced few or no results

▶▶ Unclear objectives

▶▶ Unsure who should be in the meetings

▶▶ No task list

▶▶ Unsure who is running the show

▶▶ Unclear agenda

▶▶ Vague timelines

▶▶ No business objectives

▶▶ Confusion on technology choices

▶▶ Content soon defined as a "four letter word"

AwwaRF had not been through this intense a process before. Their most recent Web site was completed by an internal Web developer, who had put together a well-constructed project plan, but this was to be the organization's first step into building a complete and highly complex, Web plan. Unlike many organizations, AwwaRF's recent experience had been positive, so they went into the Analysis Phase with optimism and enthusiasm. Many organizations view this process as a nightmare, though. They often begin the new project nervous and uncomfortable, unsure of how the deliverables will be completed and if they will be completed on time and on budget.

LACK OF A PLAN

If you were fortunate and your redesign went through smoothly, count yourself lucky. AwwaRF was one of the lucky ones, having an intelligent, well organized, internal Web developer and a qualified Web vendor (XploreNet) to walk them through the entire Web project. For many firms, the reality is that most redesigned Web sites do not achieve a high level of satisfaction. According to Robert McGlouton, Vice President of SatisfactionWorks, a company that performs satisfaction surveys after Web redesigns, "Communication is an important key while understanding all the expectations of all parties involved."

The biggest obstacle is the lack of a plan. If the site you have isn't the one you wanted, then you did not have a proper Web plan. As the old saying goes "if you don't know where you're going, any where will do." Sure, you may have had a basic project plan last time, but you may have overlooked how the new site or application would fit in with all your other Web strategies. AwwaRF now had to look at the business reasons, creating user profiles, and understand how their brand awareness would be affected by their new site. They were forced to match the business objectives, which included increasing the number of subscribers, improving value to subscribers, and improving online collaboration between consultants, to the Web strategies. Similar to getting that painful root canal, the situation can be seen more favorably if you know what the procedure is, you trust the team doing it, and you understand the anticipated outcome.

If you haven't used a Web plan before, now is your chance to get started. Put those bad experiences behind you and smile. Once you understand what went right and wrong the last time, you can make sure the next time is a successful experience, and even perhaps, a pleasant one.

Your Purpose (1.2)

Purpose:	Evaluating your reasons for a new Web project
Key Points:	Understanding the purpose of the project and answering the simple question, "Why are we doing this?" will help a great deal. This is the section where you begin to understand the

> business reasons for the project and what will harm or help the process.

If you're thinking about a Web site redesign or building a new Web application and you're having some hesitation, it may be because you haven't answered the first critical question: Why are we doing this?

AwwaRF knew their purpose, making the initial meetings and discussions straightforward. You may have many reasons, including leading-edge brand image, selling more products, qualifying prospects, improving customer service, creating more interaction, or improving internal communication. The purpose for your new Web project may involve all of these reasons, but have you identified them, put them in writing, and prioritized their importance? The purpose of AwwaRF's new site was to make them the number one, best known, world leader in water research. Their purpose was written down, emphasized, and digested over and over.

THE PURPOSE

You've probably had a Web site for a while and now you're asking "What is the purpose?" You might have put up the first one or redesigned it a few times because every one else did—competitors, vendors, customers, etc. When we've asked new clients what the purpose of the current site was they often reply "every one has a Web site". Did you ever ask why? Not only the purpose of the site, but why are you redesigning it? It's important for you to know. Keep reading and you'll find out why it's important for you to know why.

THE SMART TEST

You may understand some of the reasons listed in the first, moving forward with a redesign, but have you put the SMART test to them? The SMART test comes from the self-help industry and is used to measure goals. Are your reasons for the redesign or new application Specific, Measurable, Agreed upon, Realistic, and Time based? You should also add Clear, Concise and Fundamental (we'll call this CCF for now). If you can't plan and then measure it, don't do it.

FIND OPPORTUNITIES

You need to comprehend opportunities that are either obvious or hidden. AwwaRF identified three key competitors and during the Analysis Phase, learned to understand what made them similar and different. They strived to find out why a water utility would choose them over the key competitors.

Follow AwwaRF's lead and look at what some of your competitors are doing on the Web. Perform a basic competitive analysis. Is what they're doing making sense? Do they have some good ideas? Are they developing innovative digital ways to sell their products or services? In addition, look for the hidden opportunities by asking your current customers for their opinions (we'll get into this in more detail later in the book). As you identify opportunities and define the purpose, ask some key questions like:

- ▸▸ Will we increase the number of new clients?
- ▸▸ Will existing clients see an improvement in customer service?
- ▸▸ Is the redesign part of a new branding campaign?
- ▸▸ Is this the time to create more differentiation between us and our competitors?
- ▸▸ Are we launching a new product or service?
- ▸▸ Do we have a realistic budget?
- ▸▸ Will it help our employees to be more efficient?
- ▸▸ Are there alternatives to building the new application(s)?

According to Jacob Nielson of the Nielson Norm Group, redesigned sites and Web applications have a low success rate and the many areas measured for improvement see only slight increases. There are many causes for a redesign to take place, but typically companies implement the changes just for the sake of change. They may briefly think about all the reasons listed in the first paragraph in this Module, but they don't have a real plan or understand strategies they are trying to accomplish. Change, for the sake of change, is not the best reason. In fact, if only one key reason exists, for example, competitive pressures but nothing else don't do it. If the real purposes are not established, then the project is dead before it is born.

AwwaRF's redesign was successful because their purpose was clearly defined and matched to overall company goals. In fact, the site won two APEX awards in 2004 for best redesign and most improved internal Web pages. If you can *objectively* answer the "why" question then your next Web project has an outstanding chance of success.

Real Goals (1.3)

Purpose:	Understand all the goals of the project and how they match your business and sales objectives

Key Points:　Evaluate the goals that matter—increased sales, revenue, profit, and cost reduction. After establishing the business goals, turn your attention to project goals. Write the goals down and then match them to the new project.

How many firms put their Web goals in writing and perform a reality test on each one? According to the Franklin-Covey Organization, goals are more than seven times more likely to be accomplished if written down on paper. We often hear prospects say "We don't need to know the details and/or flush out the goals; we just need a great looking site that increases revenue," or "just make it work". We frequently respond by saying "What if the goals are met with a poorly designed site that looks terrible? What if the site has no unique tools, but quadruples revenue? You probably look as confused as they often did.

The following brief example will help clarify the point. The site www.google.com, does not meet any of the definitions of a flashy, interactive, or complex Web site. However, for Google the purpose is to get people into the search process as quickly and simply as possible. Their recent IPO suggests that their site and business objectives are working. The bottom line is that you must first detail the business and project goals in the Web plan, brainstorming on as many goals as possible, and then prioritizing them in order of importance.

SWOT ANALYSIS

AwwaRF came to XploreNet with eight site and project goals. They had spent time reviewing and understanding the importance of each goal. XploreNet helped them prioritize and flush out the details by performing a Web SWOT analysis (SWOT stands for Strengths, Weaknesses, Opportunities, Threats). The strengths of your current site might range from a well-designed "look and feel," to quality content. Weaknesses typically range from bad design to a complete lack of calls to action. Opportunities like repeat sales can be uncovered when you complete the Analysis Phase of the Web plan. Threats are all over the place—what do your competitors' Web sites look like and how good is their content? For example, do they have a shopping cart and your site states "call to order"? The SWOT analysis will help you prioritize the key goals and eliminate unnecessary or ineffective objectives.

BUSINESS GOALS

Business goals include sales increases, cost reductions, brand evaluations and improvements, etc. Real business goals for a new Web project must be objective, quantifiable, and realistic. If you think that the new site will mean a 40 percent increase in traffic and revenue then, are you thinking logically? How will you get there? What other strategies will be affected? How will you track and measure the results? Indeed, many firms have their heads in the clouds when it comes to the Web. Your goals may or may not be realistic, but ask yourself as you're going through the process, "Are we in Fantasyland or is this truly possible?

Some common categories for business goals include:

Increasing online sales

▸▸ The challenging part of this goal is that many firms do not have good records of their online sales. If you do, then what type of growth do you want to see? How many new visitors will it take to get there? How will the online store be built to achieve your goals? If the site visitor can buy online from you, then the redesign and accompanying tools must enhance that experience. Once you put the right tracking processes in place, the goals are easily quantifiable—how many new sales, how much increase in revenue, how much reduction in internal staffing, etc.

Increasing requests for information and/or appointments

▸▸ This goal could have a direct affect on revenue. The key is to understand the average lifetime value of a customer. These numbers should be quantifiable. For example, currently we're getting 10 leads a week and the new site will increase the requests to 20. By hitting our goals we'll increase revenue by100 percent.

Increasing brand value

▸▸ If the focus of your firm is delivering offline services or products, then your site must enhance your marketing and public relations plans. This is difficult to measure; however, performing usability testing during the development process to understand your brand value will create a measurement baseline. Then, once the site is launched, perform a follow-up usability test where the testing group again rates your brand. You may be able to identify something like, "We've improved our visitor satisfaction by 75 percent%," or "Prospects are demonstrating more brand recognition".

Improving customer satisfaction and/or decreasing internal staffing costs

▸▸ The belief has always been that a Web presence can improve the level of customer support. It can, if it's done correctly. However, if your site must provide a high level of support to the visitor, then the tools on the site must be highly sophisticated. How do you measure the success rate here? Usability testing, online surveys, traffic increases to certain sections, or specific customer service tools are solid goal areas.

Publishing Information
▸ If your site publishes valuable information—downloadable articles, newspaper articles, training information, etc, you'll want to establish goals like increases in fee subscriptions, increases in total subscriber base, and/or increases in pay-per-download revenue.

PROJECT GOALS

Project goals go hand in hand with business goals and include budget restraints, timelines, team members, development issues, technology options, etc. AwwaRF was different from most firms who typically have a single project goal. AwwaRF had several project goals and used them to flush out the details of the scope of work. Project goals tend to be simpler to define than the business goals of the new Web project.

Example project goals include:
▸ Completing the project in three months, in six months, etc.
▸ Completing the project for a $100,000 budget, $90,000 budget, etc.
▸ Accomplishing weekly communication and updates
▸ New design complete in four weeks, in three weeks, etc.
▸ Database completed by March 1, or May 1, etc.
▸ 50 percent increase in traffic from Google, etc.
▸ 30 percent improvement in email click-through rates

PRIORTIZE GOALS

XploreNet helped AwwaRF determine the goals that mattered most to the organization. We helped them focus on three to four main goals and a few subcategories of goals. You may need to build the site or tool around the delivery of these points to the visitor. Clearly defined goals will assist you in understanding your main priorities and maintaining perspective as you run into project obstacles or challenges. Of course, you can't have everything. So, what will be most critical and what fits the long term company plans?

As most business owners and executives know, goals are always the key to success. No matter what the end Web goals, they must first be realistic, agreed upon, scheduled, and written out in your Web plan.

Personnel Involved (1.4)

Purpose:	Understand what members of your staff need to participate in the project and what their project functions might be
Key Points:	This section covers the specific team members involved in your redesign or implementation committee. Understand which personnel should be involved, their level of involvement, and their project purpose.

A true Web plan is put together by several members of your organization. Each participant on the Web team has specific strategies and goals in mind. It has been XploreNet's experience that committees of 12 people can work out well, while two-person development committees may result in a fiasco. Usually when we begin a Web project, the client is often not sure who should be involved in the process. Assembling the right team and understanding how your team will work with an outsourced vendor <u>before</u> you get started; can greatly affect the success of your next Web project.

TALENT INVENTORY

If you have an internal Web team, then you probably have most of your players available. You should have the following skill sets: strategic person, marketing coordinator, project manager, front-end development (look-and-feel person, graphics, etc.), and a technical person (HTML, complex programming, server issues, etc.). If you are missing team personnel or have team personnel where they should not be, you're in for a rude awakening. You will likely end up with poor quality commentary, unfocused meetings, missing resources and above all, <u>lost time and money</u>. These same problems arise when you have too many people involved. We've seen committees of 12 to 15 people where tangents and alternative agendas take center stage. This is not an effective and efficient team.

If you're using an outsourced vendor, then access the talents of both your internal team and the vendor's team. XploreNet and AwwaRF created a project team as if it were a combined company. Both organizations understood each person's role in the team, clearly defined that role, and disclosed all expectations. We worked together to identify what talents were missing and how to fill the gap accordingly.

PERSONNEL PLAN

AwwaRF was fortunate because they had an outstanding internal Web master and several willing committee participants. Their Web committee consisted of 10 people from different divisions with very specific goals in mind. Like AwwaRF, if you have the right players (it can be two to 10—try not to have more than 12 if possible) involved, the process runs smoothly and makes sense. The rule of thumb is that if you are a medium to large firm then you should have three to 10 people involved. They must be decision makers, who understand your overall company objectives, the services/products, and the core values. Typically this includes the President/owner, CIO, CTO, CFO, VP or Director of Marketing, Sales Manager/rep, Marketing Executive/outsourced Marketing vendor, office manager/customer service/operations, and IT employee/outsourced vendor.

If your firm is a small business, make sure you have at least two people involved. If you're solo, have a partner company, networking contact, vendor and/or customer involved in the process. If you can only have one other person involved, make it a customer. This person will help you understand why they chose you and how your new Web presence can help attract more great clients. You will receive incredibly valuable insight you never thought was possible to achieve.

The process of understanding who should be involved in the project and, knowing which talents to use and when to use them can be complicated and difficult. However, if you take the time to understand the process and identify the key players, you then already have a 50 percent greater chance of success. The strategy meetings with AwwaRF were productive because the right personnel were engaged at the right time.

Define Success (1.5)

Purpose:	What is a successful Web project to you? Establish a definition of success.
Key Points:	In this section you'll want to write down what success looks like for your Web project. Be as detailed as possible.

If someone walked into your company and told you that they were considering your product/service, but they also told you what information they thought was most important for them to decide to buy from you right now, instead of your competition, wouldn't you make sure that they received the information they needed? Most companies work hard to keep existing customers and to gain new ones. Yet how much time and money is wasted on addressing the *perceived* needs instead of the *known* needs of both existing and potential customers?

GOLD MINE

Almost every company with a Web site is sitting on a gold mine of information that could tell what their customers' true needs are, what is important to the customers, and what sales/marketing language is most effective for getting the customers to buy from them, instead of their competition. AwwaRF had customer surveys and traffic reports filled with important statistics. They needed to put the information into a Web analytics format. Web analytics is a term used to describe the ability to measure and interpret information about how online visitors behave.

Here's an eye opening statistic: recent studies have shown that on average, nearly 80 percent of potential purchasers of goods and services believe that going to a company's Web site is an important part of the decision making process. If you have a Web site, what is it telling that 80 percent of your potential purchasers? If you don't have a Web site, or the site is poorly planned and constructed, how will that negatively impact the impression of your company? Will you be perceived as "real"? Think about all those potential customers looking at your Web site as they try to decide if they'll buy from you. Do you know what information is critical for them to make that purchase decision?

Let's think about your Web site's visitors in a more traditional sales funnel manner (see Figure 1).

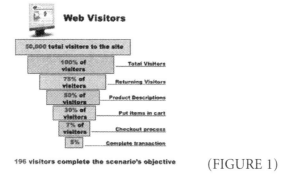

Web Visitors

50,000 total visitors to the site

100% of visitors	Total Visitors
75% of visitors	Returning Visitors
50% of visitors	Product Descriptions
30% of visitors	Put Items in cart
7% of visitors	Checkout process
5%	Complete transaction

196 visitors complete the scenario's objective   (FIGURE 1)

Most salespeople look at the universe and decide what type of individuals or companies might buy from them (suspects). Then, they ask themselves, who is more likely to need what I offer? By breaking down that universe into more specific groups or targets, the salesperson has just defined groups that are more likely to buy from them (prospects). From these prospects they focus again on those that have a more pressing need, and these people become qualified <u>leads</u>.

In the Web-enabled world, your Web site actually knocks out one layer of the traditional sales funnel. Everyone that comes to your Web site does so *voluntarily*. Rather exciting to think these visitors are specifically going to you to fulfill their needs. Somehow they have been enticed to sit down, turn on a computer, find your Web address, and look at your Web site. Why? Because they're likely considering buying from you and they want more information.

Now, let's look at the other side. Most visitors to your Web site know on some level, what information they are looking for. Therefore your Web site should be clearly organized, copy should be concise and to the point, with standard terms used for the navigation (References, About Us, Contact, Pricing, Solutions, Services, Examples, etc...(Navigation should be obvious and consistent throughout the site).

So let's stop for a moment and check where we are. About 80 percent of the people thinking about buying from you will probably look at your Web site. The mere act of going to your Web site indicates that they have some level of interest in what you have to offer. The next question is, "Do you know what information they want?" This is the critical information that will compel them to buy from you instead of your competition.

MARKETING TOOL

Your Web site is an incredible marketing tool. Not only can you quickly change your Web site, but also those that visit your Web site are qualified leads. Here's a piece of information most people don't have: everything that happens on your Web site can be tracked, measured, and analyzed—this is Web analytics. AwwaRF had been tracking some of the site users, but needed usable information. They had to determine how people found the foundation, what marketing/sales language was most effective, and what type of information their different subscriber groups (customer segments) needed to have to make a purchase decision. This is extremely valuable information; too bad most companies don't take advantage of such a gold mine. In Section 1.6 we take a look at how to access the information, how to interpret the data, and how to put both the information and insight into action. In the end, you'll have a definition of success and an established return on investment (ROI).

Establish ROI (1.6)

Purpose:	Understand and articulate the ROI and tracking processes
Key Points:	Establish Web metrics that match sales and business objectives. Evaluate various Web tools to make sure your Web

> analytics are reasonable and simple. Create systems to quantify everything you do. Include as much data as possible in your Web plan.

By now you've heard all the buzzwords around Web analytics, but what does it really mean? It is absolutely necessary to establish a baseline so you can track and measure online behavior, over time. In fact, you must be able to quantify everything you are doing, in order to get a true return on investment. XploreNet helped AwwaRF establish a baseline to quantify success, the steps towards which success could be achieved over time. During the Analysis Process, AwwaRF recognized how much a visitor meant to the organization in terms of life-time value and what the average cost would be to get the visitor to use the site tools. As you look at your Web presence, if you know that for every 100 visitors, you get one sale at an average sale price of $200, you obviously want to improve the ratio of visitors to sales (sometimes called a conversion rate). So how do you do it? There are two categories for ROI—business objectives and user behavior metrics. Business objectives include sales figures, revenue goals, and profit targets, while user behavior incorporates Web traffic and statistical analysis.

ROI

Return on Investment or ROI is a popular term these days. Have you sat through a vendor presentation where ROI wasn't discussed? ROI is the central force for the success of any company, no matter how large or small. You will need to establish ROI goals for your new Web project. Establish breakeven points and points of no return (When do we stop investing in the site and look at a new strategy?) During the first strategy session with AwwaRF, XploreNet discussed what would be the target for increased subscriptions and renewals (sales revenue). It was necessary to understand how much profit could be tied to the new project. We detailed these goals in the Web plan.

In order to study behavior, you probably already have the fundamental building blocks to understanding how and why your visitors behave the way they do. Every Web site visitor generates a history of the visit that tracks each page seen, how long each page was displayed, etc. All of these visits are compiled and stored in a Web site's log files. In essence, the log files are a historical record of how each visitor interacted with your Web site. Your Web host probably has a few months of your Web site's historical log files. These are usually saved on a month-by-month basis. Many hosting companies offer monthly reports that show standardized reports regarding your Web-site. This information varies based upon the Web analytics service your Web hosting company subscribes to. But, almost always, you'll at least have the following information:

- Total Visits
- Average Visits per Day
- Average Page Views per Visit
- New Visitors
- Total Page Views
- Average Page Views per Day
- Average Hits per Visit
- Repeat Visitors
- Total Hits
- Average Bytes per Day
- Average Length of Visit

USING THE DATA

Now that you have the information, how do you put it to work? One month's information doesn't mean too much. What really counts is the trends established and verified in the month-to-month reports. AwwaRF's three-month data trends showed that most visitors used the pages found in the project center. If you notice that your total number of visitors is declining, and the average length of the visit is also declining, check your sales. Often, sales will have dropped within the same time frame.

This leads us to interpreting and applying the information from that data. If you're fortunate enough to have access to more comprehensive reporting solutions, here are some of the areas that you should consider investigating:

- Top path analysis
- Key search words/phrases
- Referring URLs

Web analytics or metrics are industry term "buzz words" to describe the process of quantifying Web activities and objectives. Some real world examples may help you see how you can use this information:

Example 1: You use your Web site to showcase your work and generate sales leads (your Web site has two goals, show examples of your work, and have people contact you because they are considering using your services or purchasing your products). Using Total Page Views, Average Page Views per Visitor, New and Repeat Visitors, let's look at how these numbers trend over a 3-month period.

Do the numbers for each stay the same or fluctuate? More than likely, the numbers change month to month:

Total Page Views	Total Page Views will give you a rough idea of how much activity is on your Web site.
The Average Page Views	The Average Page Views per Visitor indicate how involved your visitors are with your Web site. If the number is less than 2, it could mean that most visitors are confused/bored/uncertain after arriving at your homepage and don't know what to do next (this assumes, of course, you have at least 10 pages to your Web site). Most visitors see, or don't see, something that makes them leave your Web site.
New and Repeat Visitors	Let's add New and Repeat Visitors. Do you have more New Visitors acting this way? If so, something on your Web site within those first two pages is driving them away from you, make sure your links work, your copy is clear, and you have a defined path/goal for visitors to take next (e.g. click here for examples, click here for more information, click here for references). More than likely, your visitors don't know where to go next. It's your job to lead them.

Example 2: You sell products or services online. By analyzing information from the Navigational Path report, key search words/phrases, number of visitors, and your total sales, you can figure out who (Google, Yahoo, MSN, etc.) is bringing you the best traffic. Here, we define best traffic as those that buy from you, not just those that visit your Web site. By working backwards, we look at the total number of people that saw your "Thanks for your purchase" page (from the Navigational Path report). We then see the pages that most of those people viewed before they saw that page. All we're doing is recreating the most popular pages viewed (and in which o sequence) on your Web site. Notice which pages people used to arrive at the "Thanks for your purchase" page. Here are the Web pages that directly impact your sales. What is on those pages? Whatever page it is that information is crucial in driving your visitors to buy from you.

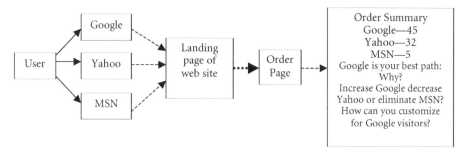

<u>Example 3</u>: Using the same report, look at the top paths. How long are they, and where do they end (at what page)? You may be loosing visitors along the way to your "Thanks for your purchase" page because of something you're not providing. Look at the pages and see what topics they discuss, what those pages have in common. Is the copy clear? Are links working to the next page? Have you clearly outlined the next step you want your visitors to take? We keep looking back through the sales funnel until we arrive at your home page.

Establishing ROI is critical to any Web project. You will need to understand some basic metrics set up and then match your business goals to the metrics. It is only at this point that you will have a real Return on Investment.

Choosing A Firm (1.7)

Purpose:	Develop a game plan for choosing the right Web firm

Key Points:	Understanding the best fit for your firm's size, goals, and budget is of critical importance. What are the characteristics that make sense? What type of firm is <u>not</u> a good choice?

Now that you understand the overall objectives and you have the right players in place, it's time to choose the development company. Choosing the right Web firm is critical to your company's Web project success. Choose wisely. The company you choose can either make or break your Web plan.

There are probably 10,000 or more Web firms in the United States, divided between large enterprise integrators, small to medium sized Web shops, and numerous independent contractors. Picking the right firm from all these choices can be like playing Russian roulette. AwwaRF simplified the process by preparing interview questions with a clear understanding how the chosen firm would help the organization complete its custom Web plan.

FIRST TIME

If you've never worked with a Web firm before, you need a Web plan. If you've never worked with a Web shop the cost estimates you receive may give you sticker shock. In fact, you may be tempted to find a low cost, independent developer. If you've had a good experience with this type of vendor, then count yourself fortunate and keep using that vendor. However, if you've gone this route, you were more likely to have had a bad experience. You've probably seen the bad and the ugly. Picking the right company is about matching your strategies and project goals to the firm that has the best chance of delivering.

DO YOUR HOMEWORK

As you go through the process of picking the right Web firm, **do your homework.** Scott Smeester from TIDF helps clients determine their IT and technology needs. He recommends you understand the following before you engage a firm: (Most of these questions are answered in Modules 1 and 2 of your Web plan)

▸▸ What do you want to accomplish with your Web site?

▸▸ What are your goals for this project?

▸▸ Why will your visitors benefit by coming to your site?

▸▸ How often will this site be changing? (i.e. content, structure, graphics)

▸▸ What makes your company competitive?

▸▸ What does your company do?

▸▸ What will determine if the Web project is a successful investment or not?

▸▸ What are your goals for this project?

▸▸ What is the level of computer experience of your audience?

▸▸ In your opinion, what makes a good site and what makes a poor site?

▸▸ Do you have a budget set aside? How much have you allotted for each strategy?

▸▸ What is your Internet experience?

▸▸ Do you have a budget set aside for monthly hosting and maintenance?

▸▸ Do you have graphics that will need to be developed?

▸▸ How much of your content is completed?

RECEIVING REFERRALS

As we mentioned before, there are numerous choices in Web firms. So where do you begin? Your best bet is to begin with a referral. Ask associates, friends, professional contacts, etc. which firms they've had good experiences with. AwwaRF found XploreNet by asking the company that performed their offline marketing for a referral. When you have identified a few (typically three or four is sufficient) take them through the full interview process.

INTERVIEW PROCESS

AwwaRF looked at 12 companies and interviewed four of them by organizing two different question and answer sessions. They wanted to make sure the prospective firms and their team could ask questions of one another, thoroughly evaluating which firm would be the best match. XploreNet asked project and business-related questions that helped our team assess where AwwaRF was in the process and how we could take them from point A to Z (most questions will be easy for you to answer if have done your homework).

Once we understood their business, they needed to know what we could do for them. AwwaRF understood the technology options, XploreNet's approach, XploreNet's methods to get more value for their budget limitations, and the best type of implementation. According to Istudio, you should ask to see examples of a consultant's successful Web projects and attempt to answer the following questions:

▸▸ Does their own Web site match their objectives?

▸▸ Do their case studies match some of your needs?

▸▸ Are there errors on their site or broken links?

▸▸ Is the content on their site relevant?

▸▸ How many projects, similar to yours, have they completed?

▸▸ Do they have information about their processes and does it make sense?

▸▸ Who are their team members?

▸▸ Do they have the experience to help you?

▸▸ How did you find the firm?

THE BEST MATCH

After taking the prospective Web firms through the interview process, look for the following information from their answers. Look for the firm that:

You can create a relationship with

▸▸ Ask if they have relationships with their clients that are more than three years old.

Has experience with projects having similar goals to your project

▸▸ If your goal is to create a site to develop additional sales channels, ask what their experience is in this endeavor.

Has a strong outsourcing/referral model

▸▸ Don't buy into the one-stop shop. It doesn't exist. The company that "does it all" does none of it well.

Has been in the Internet industry for at least five years

▸▸ How much can you afford to pay for their inexperience?

Has a clearly defined process for Web projects
➡ What are the different steps, from beginning to end, to complete a project? What makes it successful?

Has a real business location
➡ What happens if your developer is not committed to the business? Having a business location shows a strong level of commitment.

HELP WITH YOUR WEB PLAN

Your most important step in choosing a firm: determine how they will assist you in developing your Web plan. XploreNet came to AwwaRF with a Web plan outline and showed how the project would be successful upon implementing the strategies of the plan. If you don't have a Web plan, the firm you work with should help you implement one. If you have a detailed Web plan, match your strategies to the firm you choose.

Strategy Meetings (1.8)

Purpose:	Understand how to organize and run a successful strategy meeting
Key Points:	Understand the agenda for the meetings and what the end results should be, upon completion. You should have a plan going in to the meeting and know what areas will be potential stumbling blocks.

According to Mike Ewart-Smith of the Whitegrove Group, "If the formulation of strategy is not being undertaken in strategy meetings, there is probably no strategy at all." A strategy meeting for your new Web project should cover the business strategies, business goals, project goals, and other key components discussed in previous sections of this book.

XploreNet guided AwwaRF through four strategy sessions totaling 14 hours. We utilized our experience of conducting more than 200 strategy sessions, helping AwwaRF detail the agenda, and hit the most important priorities. Our unique agenda format helped AwwaRF to realize an effective Analysis Phase plan. Your strategy sessions will be successful if you have a proper agenda and understand some of the "dos" and "don'ts" of the meeting format.

AGENDA

First, establish the agenda. Make sure you consider *all* the opportunities and issues that must be covered, in order to build the foundation for your project's success. This includes not only the main goals, but also all the different departmental issues. If you are a large firm, you will need to include several areas. If you're small, the issues may be smaller. Give the meeting a catchy name that will excite the participants, but make the purpose and goals of the meeting apparent. The tag line of the meeting should be something interesting, challenging, and significant. Accentuate the importance of the meeting and persuade participants to buy into the excitement. For example: ACME Company Web Strategy Meeting: Developing the Path to Success for 2005.

If you are to head the meeting with your own team, communicate with the lead consultant of the development company on what you want to see covered and the key strategies that should be defined by the end of the meeting. Make sure you gage the time necessary to cover all topics—you may have to organize two or more meetings to completely cover every detail. Next, create a list of all participants and communicate with them to understand what topics they would like to cover. Emphasize the importance of the meeting and why they must participate.

At the end of the book we provide a strategy session guideline. Be sure you prepare copies of the agenda in detail, being careful not to include too much information, but enough to accomplish the priorities. Create a statement of purpose and an overview of steps to illustrate to the participants how the team will get from A to Z. After this meeting, you will know what you want to cover, the necessary time commitment, what materials to use, and who will be involved. How do you make the process work?

DOS AND DON'TS

The key question becomes, "How do we run a successful strategy session?" Here are a few tips for the process:

▸▸ **Do** utilize flip charts and hand outs

▸▸ **Do** have some type of tool to illustrate the flow chart of the project

▸▸ **Do** make sure you have a high speed Internet connection

▸▸ **Do** use PowerPoint via a projector

▸▸ **Do** plan for a short break, once every hour

▸▸ **Do** tell participants to turn off cell phones, PDAs, etc.

▸▸ **Don't** run over the scheduled time period

▸▸ **Do** introduce the team members (unless every one knows each other) and discuss their reason for attending the meeting

▸▸ **Don't** let other issues get onto the agenda—create an "other issues funnel" (meaning this is where issues that fall outside of the agenda will be listed and can be taken care of outside of the meeting or at the next meeting)

▸▸ **Don't** let one particular agenda item take more than first estimated. If the issues needs more time, delegate the issue to someone who can take care of it outside of the meeting

▸▸ **Don't** let a few participants monopolize all topics

▸▸ **Do** take notes and record an audio of the meeting

▸▸ **Do** summarize at the end of the meeting

▸▸ **Do** set up the parameters for the next meeting

A successful strategy session should cover all the topics we have covered in Phase 1 and begin laying the groundwork for Phase 2.

Creating a Creative or Technology Brief (1.9)

Purpose:	Understand the key elements of a creative and/or a technology brief
Key Points:	In this section you will learn the elements of a creative brief and a technology brief. You will understand how to write one and what it should and should not include.

A creative brief and a technology brief give an overview of your project from separate angles. XploreNet assisted AwwaRF in completing a creative brief, covering "look and feel" issues, user goals, usability, navigation, etc., while the technology brief helped AwwaRF with the technical options: technical skill levels, technical platforms, and hosting environments. Both briefs help describe the goals of the project, just as the Web plan describes the Web strategies. When properly developed, these briefs enhance the scope of work.

CREATIVE BRIEF

Taking a closer look at the creative brief, the document outlines the objectives, perceptions, positioning, audience, communication strategy, and assumptions for the project. The creative brief details the creative concepts the development team intends to implement. What does it look like?

We have included one in the Web Plan in Module 5 as a template for your use. The first part of the brief covers the project summary, followed bygeneral project information, goals, and relevant background information for the Web project. The initial paragraph should be a statement overview of the project as a whole. This part is similar to an executive summary and covers both short and long term goals.

The next section covers perception/tone/guidelines, and facilitating how your target audience should respond to your new online presence. This paragraph covers the details of what the target audience thinks and feels about your company and the site. In addition, you will need to detail what you want your visitors to think and feel. For example, it should include adjectives that describe the way the site and your company should be perceived by the target audience. Finally, you should cover the specific visual goals the site should convey.

The third part includes the communication strategy. At the end of this section you will understand how to convince the target audience to make a purchase decision with you. Important questions include that of the overall message you are trying to convey to your target audience. How will you convey the overall message? It is at this point, you will need to identify the stages of development (if appropriate) used to execute your goals.

Lastly, communicate how you intend to measure the success of your Web project. This section covers an evaluation of the existing site to compare to the new one and the competitive positioning. The final section deals with the targeted message. You must answer the questions, "How are we different from our competition and what factors will make us a success?" Detail the factors that make you different and what specifically sets you apart from your competition. You must state a concise word or phrase that will appropriately describe the site once it is launched. This should include the calls to action and overall brand the user experiences.

TECHNOLOGY BRIEF

The technology brief is often overlooked. This document details the technical options and processes the development team intends to utilize. A technology brief fills in the gaps left by using only a creative brief. The additional information includes technology options and the process necessary to implement the creative brief. In other words, how will the technical or functional side of the project work in conjunction with the creative side? This is where you create a balance between cool, neat, and new technology, and the user's ability to use it and make use of it.

The technology brief defines the platforms to be used and the skill required to use them. It also aids in the functional requirements. In fact, many sites and applications look great, but are useless as far as the user is concerned. The developer may have overlooked how the graphics and content will fit in properly with the functional requirements.

The creative brief and technology brief are key components to planning your project and they must fit properly in the blue print section of your Web plan.

COMPLETION OF MODULE 1

The AwwaRF project and resulting Web plan was successful because the Analysis Phase covered in Module 1 was well organized, detailed, and complete. In fact, SatisfactionWorks completed a survey of the AwwaRF users after the redesign, finding that the redesign achieved a 93 percent approval rating—the highest rating they had ever seen.

The Analysis Phase is different for every firm. If you've dedicated the time to complete the analysis, you are well on your way to a successful Web project. Be sure to refer to Module 5 for the outline and details of a properly constructed Web plan.

MODULE 2: BLUE PRINT

2.0 Blue Print

This module discusses the next phase of understanding how your Web projects fit into your Web plan. This is the point where the Web strategies begin to take life and meet in the middle, with the project goals. Once you have completed this module, you will understand the details of your project. As you learn about blue printing, you will quickly understand whether your Web strategies are on life support or whether they are dead. Companies that successfully implement the correct blue print typically build a truly great Web project. This is where the theories and ideas become real. The blue print should detail the anticipated number and style of visitors, personalization issues, relevant calls to action, the scope of work, technology options, content requirements, initial design thoughts, usability, technical personnel involved, and future technology plans.

Most modern Web sites do not meet the criteria of *effective* Web projects because they did not have a good blue print. They completed pages without understanding the purposes of the finished product.

Most books and Web firms cover a Blue Print Phase strictly from their point of view, completing a scope of work. This is an important step in the process; however, you must understand who is using the site, how they use it, and what you can do to keep them using it. We suggest that the blue print serve as your reality check. This process enables the executives to connect their strategies with the finished product and the marketing personnel to make sure their initiatives are being met.

CASE STUDY

Breakthrough Management Group, Inc. (BMG) is the leading provider of Six Sigma training, support and consulting services designed to help organizations achieve breakthrough level performance. BMG prides itself on its top quality training programs for Six Sigma Black Belts, Green Belts, Master Black Belts, Champions and all levels of management. Training classes are available through public classes and on-site programs as well as through BMG's Web-based platform.

The existing BMG Web site, located at www.bmgi.com, did not meet the credentials of an industry leader. Wendy St. Clair, the company's VP of Marketing, realized that the Web presence was a key component in the company's continued growth and success. BMG looked at several Web firms, narrowing the list down to four finalists and ultimately choosing XploreNet to implement their new Web plan. They chose XploreNet because of our combined experience in both Web site graphic design and database work. Furthermore, XploreNet's depth and breath of knowledge in building complex, database-driven Web sites showed BMG that XploreNet had the ability to help them develop a site that met their growing ecommerce and brand building needs, concurrently.

XploreNet put a Web plan together that included a detailed blue print, creation of a user profile, flushing out calls to action, completing a detailed scope of work, confirming technology options, organizing content areas, performing usability testing, and building towards future growth of the company.

BMG's ability to complete the Blue Print Phase proved critical in the successful redesign of their Web presence.

Understanding Visitors (2.1)

Purpose:	Understand the visitors that will use your Web project once it's complete, whether they are internal or external to the operations of your firm
Key Points:	In this section, you will learn to understand how your visitors will utilize your new tools and make logical assumptions as to their behavior, whether they are external (customers or partners) or internal (employees).

Imagine a firm that offers custom homes, but delivers the blue print on the first appointment. When it comes to the Web, many firms are getting bogged down by this problem. BMG knew that their site was not appropriate for their target audience. But they needed to have a better understanding of how users utilized their site and Web tools. They felt the lack of feedback data on their users meant that the existing site did not meet or exceed the user's expectations.

The BMG site was built mostly from the company's viewpoint, without a thorough blue print. The blue print only included the company's viewpoint, not that of the customers. This is a common problem for many firms. According to Forrester Research, only 33 percent of companies currently improve their online operations by making use of the data associated with how customers use the company's Web site. This means that nearly two-thirds of the businesses do not go into Web projects with the correct information.

USER BEHAVIOR

Professional Web-based marketing companies know that user behavior is more than just data. Simply measuring page hits, page views, click-through rates, and conversion rates is not sufficient. BMG had good traffic reporting data, but it was critical for them to have a quality understanding of their user's preferences and purchasing behavior. As most consultants agree, most traditional businesses have proven that understanding customer behavior is a key priority in keeping a customer. In fact, it can cost five to 10 times more to get a new customer then to keep a current one. So how do you avoid losing existing customers while still attracting new ones? The reality is that you need customer information to help understand what's happening with your Web presence. You need demographics, buying patterns, technical skills, and personal user preferences.

USER PROFILE

During the Analysis and Blue Print phases of the BMG project, we created a user profile that described, in as much detail as possible, the general demographics and buying tendencies of BMG users. We strived to answer the question, "What do BMG customers want from the site? For example, BMG's profile included middle managers to executive level, tending to be male in the 35 to 50 year old age range, high income, and very comfortable with the Internet. Additional demographic data might include marital status and Internet habits. In addition, you will need to have a good idea of how often and when users use the site, based on the review and establishment of metrics.

Now, what do they want from you? Later in this module we'll discuss usability, but at this point we're attempting to set up the parameters for the usability testing.

You need to answer questions like:

- ❑ Do they want to make a real-time online transaction?
- ❑ Do they want to review and edit their customer data?
- ❑ Do they want to schedule an appointment?

BMG wasn't sure what their users wanted from the site. This is a common problem because it is difficult to truly gage what exactly, your users want from your site. The findings can be subjective. However, you can make an attempt to design your ultimate user.

Typically users fall into three to six groups. BMG found three key groups. You may need to do some "digging down" to find multiple levels of users. BMG's user profile helped develop the plan for design and navigation changes. Indeed, one of their goals was to uncover the best way to motivate the site users to take the desired actions. For this, they needed answers to the following questions:

- ▸▸ Who is coming to the site?
- ▸▸ Who are our most important customers?
- ▸▸ What will they do once they get there?
- ▸▸ How do we receive them?
- ▸▸ What denotes their purchase behavior?
- ▸▸ Which online tools will generate the most profitable customers?
- ▸▸ Which products or services increase cross-sell and up-sell opportunities?
- ▸▸ What modifications will make our new Web project more customer-focused?

IDEAL CUSTOMER EXPERIENCE

Every user has a certain level of expectation when it comes to customer service. But how does a user define the ideal customer service experience on your site? When customers are utilizing the Web, it's on their own terms, but knowing what they want is crucial to your company's success. According to user research, there are five key actions in the user process:

- ▸▸ Collecting information to make the right purchasing decision
- ▸▸ Identifying their own needs
- ▸▸ Identifying the correct source to buy from
- ▸▸ Negotiating the transaction process
- ▸▸ Evaluating their own satisfaction level with the transaction

Understand what motivates the user. BMG needed to understand what their user's hot buttons were. Why would they pick BMG over many other competitors? Don't overlook the fact that just because your site or application works correctly, orders will come in.

Understanding user's behavior is difficult, but not impossible. Set up the parameters and understand the tendencies, then do the best job possible to fit their needs. BMG established a detailed, quality, user profile and the ideal user experience. This was an important step towards understanding the user's behavior on the site and creating a personalized experience.

Personalizing Your Web Presence (2.2)

Purpose: Understand how to personalize your Web presence or Web application to each user's unique tastes

Key Points: In this section, you will learn how to personalize your Web project for specific users. Based on how your users will use the site or tools, implement personal preferences.

Personalized Web sites have come about as a result of the natural progression of the Web from a push process, to a pull process. The Internet has matured and users want information on their own schedules and preferences. The challenge for any Web site owner is to match the individual tastes of each user to the site's offerings.

Can you really match each visitor's preferences when they visit your Web project? The reality is that you can match various user groups to specific offerings and in some cases personalizing each user's experience.

PERSONALIZATION DEFINED

Personalization on the Web can be defined as providing a Web experience where the user's unique tastes and actions are customized. The experience can be something as simple as providing the right search tools to something as complex as providing all current and past account activity. The actions can range from simply providing the right "look and feel" to foreshadowing the user's next moves.

Web personalization includes customized Web pages that categorize users, and matching pages to actions that make recommendations to the user. The ability to provide personalization on the Web comes from not only understanding users, but also from identifying which sections or pages users visit on your site. It is now possible for you to personalize your product message for individual visitors on a large scale. This is accomplished by tracking user behavior on your site, down to specific, single mouse clicks.

IMPLEMENTING PERSONALIZATION

The methods for accomplishing a personalized Web project are user defined preferences or group assumptions.

User defined preferences take place immediately, upon the user signing in. The user inputs information and preferences and then receives a username and password (For an example, Amazon.com performs this process). When the user returns to the site, information that has been previously stored is then delivered. Only the pages and information important to the user or that match the users previously entered guidelines are then displayed. This type of approach requires the user to give up some privacy and costs more to develop.

Group assumptions are based on the known data of typical site users, like traffic reports or product preferences, so the site owner can provide information to those groups. Assumptions can be made about what your typical user will request and what the next steps might include. Furthermore, you can provide a path to specific information by placing yourself in the position of the user: "How would I buy from you?" "What would be the next common-sense click?" This approach requires in-depth research to understand each group of preferences, but is less costly.

Personalized sites and applications help to establish an experience with a human element. By providing personalization, you prioritize the user first in your approach and in listening to their wants and needs. By understanding how to fully utilize personalization in your Web project, will come to be judged as "user friendly," based on the level of personalization you have provided.

Calls to Action (2.3)

Purpose:	Understand how to persuade your users to take your targeted action
Key Points:	In this section, we continue the blue print, analyzing what a proper call to action is, and how to implement it. The key is to have a balance between providing what the users wants and ensuring your company's goals and objectives are met, simultaneously.

You are probably familiar with the term "call to action". If you've had any prior sales training or been in business for any significant amount of time, you know what it is and how important it is to the life of a product or business. On the Web, "calls to action" become even more critical to the success of the new Web project. BMG's Web presence, like most firms on the Web, did not clearly define the calls to action. In fact, Forrester Research estimates that 45 percent of corporate sites lack a call to action or have a call to action that is confusing.

DEFINITION

A call to action on the Web is the statement or action that directs the user to complete your desired action. In other words, you must provide the appropriate information, at the right time, to enable the user to follow your guideline and ultimately make the ideal decision. BMG's user groups ranged from individuals signing up for classes to executive-level decision makers looking for an enterprise software solution. The calls to action for these groups were very different.

You have probably visited a site and wondered, "What do I do next?" You may have interest in the product or service, but you're not sure how to learn more or complete the transaction. Can you imagine going to the Airport and not seeing any signs or personnel? It would be very difficult for you to get to the right plane at the right time. BMG's users had different needs, so the calls to action needed customization, directing the user to the proper process, based on the required action. In fact, most users are left confused on many sites and typically leave because the site lacks the appropriate calls to action.

IMPLEMENTING CALLS TO ACTION

How do you implement the right calls to action? First, match the actions to the goals. Review the goals you established in Phase 1 Analysis step to come up with the appropriate ones. For example, your goals might be to increase revenue by 25 percent and increase the number of Web inquires by 15 percent. How do those goals match the calls to action?

Second, define the calls to action. BMG realized three key calls to action: (1) enterprise software prospects were to call the company, (2) those visitors searching for training were to sign up directly for the elearning class of their choice, (3) if the visitor failed to fit into one of the first two groups, that visitor would then be directed to buy products from the online shopping cart. The most obvious calls to action are: "Purchase Now," "Add to Shopping Cart," "Understand Details," "Download White Papers," "Subscribe," and others. More descriptive calls to action include: "New Visitors Start Here" or

"Returning Customer". BMG had to get the proper call to action in front of the user as soon as possible.

GUIDING THE USER

By now, you've defined what the calls to action will be. Now, it's time to explain your process to the user, answering the question "How do I do business with you?" BMG had to describe the calls to action on each page and tie each to the proper content. They would increase the satisfaction level of the user by referencing their appropriate action steps frequently.

In your situation, the call to action may be as obvious as, "This is how we do business" or "New visitors start here." You're telling the visitor to "do this" or "take this step next". For example, on the main page, include text that tells about your services and then say "for best results, fill out our Contact Us form." Then provide a link to the form from that content. You create trust and provide real customer service when the calls to action are combined with assurances like "we never sell your information" or "we offer a 100 percent money back guarantee". In the end, you're providing as much help as possible to the user so that they can do business with you.

Calls to Action are critical to the success of any Web project, but particularly for a redesign. BMG wanted to guide the user from the time the site was entered to the completion of one or all of the call to action steps.

Define Scope of Work (2.4)

Purpose:	Understand all details and sections of a properly developed scope of work
Key Points:	In this section, technical meets strategy. A clear and concise scope of work requires strong attention to detail. The scope of work document will be used to manage and implement your entire Web project. It is a combination of the information obtained in the Analysis phase and the answers derived from the creative brief and technology brief.

A scope of work is similar to a blue print for building a house. Often, it is referred to as a statement of work, working document, or project guidelines. This document is used to determine whether your ideas and goals are being properly developed. It should cover the details of design, navigation, communication, and development.

BMG came to XploreNet with a well thought out and detailed RFP, identifying the project overview and their thoughts in a rough draft scope of work. XploreNet's responsibility was to help the company confirm and enhance the scope of work to fit into the overall Web plan.

PROCESS FOR DEVELOPING THE SCOPE

We're sure you've heard of the problems associated with using a bad contractor for a bathroom remodel or room addition. This problem is often caused from a poor plan or blue print. Neither party has an identical image in mind when it comes to the details and what the final product will look like. Whether your project is complex or simple, you must have a thorough, defined scope of work.

When is the best time to draw up the scope of work? BMG was fortunate because they had a VP of Marketing who understood the importance of having some initial thoughts on the scope of work before the process began. The process for fully defining BMG's scope of work began during the Analysis Phase and was completed during the Blue Print Phase. XploreNet conducted two meetings, though one meeting is usually sufficient. During each meeting, the question and answer session helped lay out the scope of work and finished the BMG project blue print. BMG did not confirm the scope of work too early on. This often allows functional or technical requirements to be overlooked. In fact, if you wait until pages are being created during your next project, then you'll have a misunderstanding regarding the finished product.

SCOPE CONTENTS

The scope of work should include deliverables on the technical side, but also include content categories and check lists. Bullet points and flow charts cover the functional aspects of the site, while content includes key phrases, paragraphs, pictures, and processes. A correctly crafted Web project scope of work can help all personnel involved understand the details. The lack of a scope of work can cause great frustration. The scope should contain as many design and technical details as possible. A scope of work typically covers the following areas:

- ►► Goals
- ►► Deliverables
- ►► Flow chart
- ►► Assumptions
- ►► Methods for handling potential problems
- ►► Content check list
- ►► Approach
- ►► Timelines
- ►► Personnel involved
- ►► Project management process
- ►► Cost

The goals

- ►► This is very straight forward. In the Phase 1 Analysis stage you defined success and detailed the goals. Make sure you include both business and project goals. Write them down.—They can be general, (four to five areas) or each and every goal defined in detail.

Deliverables

- ►► The deliverables include all bullet points of the project and should be broken down into several areas: strategy/consultation, design/user interface, development, programming, and online marketing tactics and tools. This area should specify exactly how the database tools will be built and how they will work. In addition, describe all sections and the content required for each section.

Flowchart

- ►► The flowchart should visually demonstrate the method by which the pages and sections will flow. The basic example of this is a site map. However, a flow chart also demonstrates all the steps and paths a user can, and/or will take. Match your calls to action to the navigational flow.

Assumptions

- ►► These sections are straight forward. Keep in mind the saying "when we assume we make an a_ _ out of u and me". In this way, you will not assume too much. In a scope of work you want some assumptions. These include seemingly trivial pieces of information like the size of pages, the type of technology used, what is not included in the scope, and the financial commitments. Examples of some assumptions are that the site will be built for maximum efficiency for DSL connections or that the client is responsible for all merchant and licensing fees.

Content checklist

- ►► This list includes all areas of content, what is required, what is missing, and/or what needs to be created. Content includes all text, pictures, graphics, and database schemes.

Approach

▸▸ How is the internal Web team or outsourced partner going to accomplish the deliverables? The approach should detail step-by-step, how each part of the project will be completed.

Methods for handling potential problems

▸▸ Make sure the scope includes a method for overcoming challenges. For example, during many projects, new ideas come up that might be outside the scope—how will they be handled? Who is responsible for bringing up problems? A good scope of work details both the challenge and change management of the project. This section defines how the issues will be handled before they come up and who will be responsible for fixing them. It also helps with scope changes. Changes are a part of every scope of work and the method for discussing, pricing, and implementing the changes should be covered before you start the project.

Timelines

▸▸ A critical part of any scope of work is the timeline. Define the established milestones for the project and to whom the responsibility falls, for each one. This should include *both* the client's and vendor's tasks and deadlines.

Personnel involved

▸▸ This section should include the names, contact information, and detailed responsibilities of all personnel involved in the project. If you are using an outsourced vendor, this section should also include the vendor's background and expertise.

Project management process

▸▸ In this section detail how the project will be managed. Ask and answer the questions: "Is there a set process?" and "What tools will be used to monitor this process?" Also, will the client need a user name and password to the project management site?

Cost

▸▸ What will the costs be? Are they fixed or T&M (time & materials)? When will payments be made? Will payments be made by established deadlines or by work completed? All payments are detailed and tied to a milestone.

Payment schedule

▸▸ Develop a detailed payment plan. The plan should be based on either completion points/milestones, or dates. As long as all parties involved understand when the payments are to be made, the project should stay on schedule and finish on time.

BMG's detailed scope of work enabled the project to be successfully implemented. A correctly crafted scope reduces "scope creep issues," a term used to describe work going outside the scope, and increases the likelihood of a successful project. Many projects fail when the scope is not correct.

Technology Options (2.5)

Purpose:	Understand technology and make the right choices

Key Points:	In this section you will learn how to evaluate your technology options. Your decision will be based on budget limitations, long term goals, access to resources, and internal & external talent.

The spectrum of the World Wide Web is so large and crowded that many technological choices become lost in the shuffle. You may hear what the "experts" say about which technology to use. Hundreds of articles cover the positives and negatives of every possible technology option. Development firms have their own biases because of their own approach or internal strengths. It becomes very difficult to make the right choice for your project. How do you make the right choices?

CUSTOM NEEDS

BMG approached XploreNet requiring a Microsoft .Net programming platform. They had identified the .NET platform as the best option; however, they needed XploreNet for confirmation of that choice. The answer to making the right technology choice always comes down to you and your firm. What works best for a firm like BMG may not work for your organization. In fact, there are few, workable cookie cutter solutions. You will need to work with your entire IT and executive staff to make sure that the technology you implement for the Web fits the current platforms, staff objectives, and future plans.

CATEGORIES

Web-related technology falls into a few categories including:

❑ Graphic Development. Tools that assist with graphic creation, picture resizing, format conversion and file/graphics optimization fall into the graphic development category. Photoshop is the most commonly used graphic development program. This helps ensure the graphics, pictures, and overall design fit the page and match the brand.

❑ <u>HTML editors</u>. A second category is an HTML editor or WYSIWYG (an acronym for "what you see is what you get"). Both are tools used to create the HTML code of the Web pages. The most common program choices are Dreamweaver and FrontPage. Although many technology savvy individuals and firms use Homesite (now called Cold Fusion Studio) which is a text editor that color codes the test.

❑ <u>Programming tools</u>. The third category is programming tools which are designed for languages like Active Server Pages (ASP), .NET programming, java server pages (JSP) and PHP. These languages are used to build the database functionality in most sites and display static (HTML based) content/pages, from processing a submission form to accessing a database.

❑ <u>Databases</u>. Lastly, databases are the tools that are used to make a site truly dynamic and ever changing. They send updated information to the web site to be displayed and examples include items on sale in an ecommerce site to the current amount owed on your credit card. SQL, Oracle, MS Access, and MySQL are the most commonly used.

One way to ensure you make the right choice is to list the different categories as shown below:

Budget levels	Database Options	Programming languages	Business objectives
What can you afford and what makes the most financial sense?	Based on your budget and specific objectives which database will work? This can depend on the size of the database and expected load (how many users will be using it)	Based on the skill sets you have in-house or the firm you choose to work with, which will achieve your desired results? Also, what type of platform the site will reside on and what external systems it will interface with?	Which objectives require which technology options?
Key areas: Budget Restraints Short/Long term goals	Key areas: Hosting options Software fees	Key areas: Beginner vs. advanced skills Complex vs. simple programming	Key areas: Sales and marketing Internal communication

This diagram above shows four columns: budget levels, database options, programming languages, and business objectives. For more detail, add HTML editing and graphic development software columns. By answering the questions listed in each column you gain a strong feel for which direction to go.

CHOOSING THE RIGHT TECHNOLOGY

If you have the internal resources to identify which technology is best for your firm, use them. If you lack those resources, bring in an outside expert. BMG worked with XploreNet to make sure that the Microsoft .Net platform would work well with their goals. They required an outside professional opinion.

Here are some tips for choosing the right technology:

▶▶ Build from the strategy. Your technology choice should enhance the strategy you have begun to develop.

▶▶ Research. A little research goes a long way. Look at how other firms are improving marketing and sales through new Web technology

▶▶ One step at a time. It is not necessary to implement all the options by tomorrow. Develop a phased approach.

▶▶ Establish the budget. Set aside time & money, use part of the budget for experimentation (tools that you may or may not end up using).

▶▶ Focus on information and plans. You can increase your own power with information and connect with more customers through a well thought out plan.

▶▶ Utilize leverage.—Use technology that helps you do more, with less personnel and financial resources.

▶▶ Keep it simple. Pick the languages, the tools, and the equipment that are easy for your staff to work with.

▶▶ Use outside consultants. Get help from external resources for technical or process issues.

▶▶ Start today. The success of your firm may be defined more by your technology choices then any other factor. The mistakes you make in your early endeavors can be corrected before it's too late.

BMG was able to confirm their technology decisions because they had an understanding of all the strategic, tactical and operational factors related to their business objectives and strategy (see Module 1). They did not guess at the best option; they worked with a professional firm to identify key areas and anticipate potential problems.

Content (2.6)

Purpose:	Understand how content will be gathered or created and to whom the responsibility falls for each portion of the content
Key Points:	In this section we breakdown the critical step of Web content. A checklist of your content is required. Furthermore, you'll understand how to organize the content and deliver it in a timely manner.

After you've completed your analysis and have a good understanding of the user's behavior, the scope of work, and the technology options, you need to evaluate the content for your Web project. For our purposes, content includes text, graphics, pictures, and specific tools. Content is what makes a new site effective or ineffective. Quality content increases repeat visits and raises the level of trust with users. Content on the Web should be simple and concise. If you do not know what your visitors want, ask. A clear understanding of what your content should say (copy), and how pictures and graphics will enhance the presentation, will increase the success rate of your redesign.

IDENTIFYING PROPER CONTENT

Gathering and creating content can be one of the biggest challenges of a redesign. BMG had many user groups to which to match content, and the new content had to be in-depth and user-friendly. They knew that just utilizing the existing content and simply giving it a face-lift would be an ineffective solution. BMG's content had to be straightforward, concise, and relevant. If the content for your Web project is unclear, don't start your project. BMG knew where some of the new content would come from, but they had to match the user's goals to specific content areas. This required user feedback, and careful consideration of the responses. By taking the proper steps, you will know what type of content should be created. Use the following guideline:

Step 1: Create a content outline

Step 2: Assemble the proper materials

Step 3: Brainstorm with your staff on content categories and areas (for example—a customer service resource center)

Step 4: Think in terms of quick sound bites

Step 5: Prioritize ideas

Step 6: Create a task list

Step 7: Implement the proper content

CONTENT SOURCES

If you lack key content research services, search for sites that provide content related to your industry or topics. These are often referred to as syndicated content streams. This type of content is provided by other sites, for use on your site. You can simply place a few lines of code and content is delivered. The linked service provides the content to your site automatically with no need for maintaining the code. The content provider either charges you a fee for using the content, or they receive traffic from your site via links placed directly in the content. Interestalert.com will pay you for adding a news feed to your site. There are many free services and budget sensitive options. For example, www.7am.com provides specific news content, while www.1afm.com provides free content. Another great resource is www.yellowbrix.com, providing industry specific news and updates.

CONTENT INVENTORY

BMG identified what content would be important and created a content inventory. They utilized an excel spreadsheet (a database works well, too) to keep it organized. They created a check-list of the existing content, taking a hard look at each content area, and asked:

"What's missing?"

"What still needs to be created?"

"How long will it take to create?"

"Who needs to create it?"

WEB COPY

One of the most difficult and most important areas of content is the copy. It can be costly to create copy in time, finances, and resources. If you need to create content, designate a qualified internal staff member to do the writing or outsource the copywriting to a qualified copywriter. Poorly written copy reflects on your company's professionalism. Don't give your users any reason to doubt you. After designating the copy provider, establish a schedule to keep all personnel on track.

Writing copy for the Web is different than other marketing channels. There are several differences, but one thing remains constant—focus on the user.

What will be important to them? What will improve their chances of making a purchase decision? What type of copy will bring them back for another visit?

According to one expert, you should only write 50 percent or less of the text you would have used in hard copy. Only give your user the most pertinent information. However, be detailed when necessary, and make sure your potential customers understand the products and/or services you're offering. The Web is no place to display the full content of a book. Most users go to your site for quick, specific information—not the history of the product. Providing quick bullet lists whenever possible keeps the eye moving yet highlights key points in your copy. Keep the following tips in mind for the text of your Web project:

▸ Break pages up into short blocks. Many users become frustrated when they must page down continuously. Under no circumstances should you allow your users to become frustrated. Use different sized fonts to show important comments, and hypertext to break up pages and split long sections or tedious information. Most pages should have similar formats regarding paragraph set up, font type and size, and overall text look and feel. If customers think they've linked to a different site, then they may not come back. Web pages should have a consistent amount of text on each page.

▸ Double check, triple check, and have every resource at your fingertips look at the site for misspellings and errors. One secret to decreasing misspellings is to copy all your Web text into a Word document and hit the spell check button. Misspellings and errors cause your visitors to lose confidence in your company; Proper grammar is also critical. It can't be emphasized enough that your Web copy must be written by a qualified professional.

▸ Focus the words on customers and how your service/product helps them. Stay away from "I" and "us," and concentrate on "you" and "we." Keep text positive and forward-thinking, but not exaggerating. Offer convincing words that list the benefits and your company's enthusiasm for the business.

GRAPHICS AND PICTURES

The second category of content is graphics and pictures. First, utilize internal pictures/graphics only if they are of high quality and/or professionally done. New marketing material typically contains the right pictures and graphics. Make sure the ones you use for the Web match the offline marketing and branding packages (same feel, colors, look, consistency, etc.). Second, there are many types of libraries and online tools to capture the appropriate graphics/pictures to match your project. Perform a search on the Web with the key words "free Web graphics." You'll find plenty of libraries offering free or modestly priced graphics and pictures of the right quality. Also, invest in a subscription to an online library to purchase pictures/graphics, as you need them (www.corbis.com is a good example).

BMG realized through the blue printing process that quality content is important to visitors returning to their site and in creating the perception of expertise. There is a fine line between too little content and too much. Understanding your content needs during the Blue Print Phase will confirm whether the project schedule and timelines are realistic.

Initial Designs (2.7)

Purpose:	Establish initial designs based on the internal team's perceptions and ideas
Key Points:	Initial mock-ups will cover what the internal staff and Web vendor think are important. It is in this process where the initial usability testing begins. The final product may look nothing like these initial ideas; it's the process itself that's important.

As mentioned in the beginning of this book, redesigning a Web project can be frustrating. If the design (defined as the "look and feel' and for our purposes in this section, the "navigation") is poor, then business objectives may not be met.

XploreNet has built over 500 Web sites and applications and some tried and true theories have become very apparent. When you are blue printing the project, you must come up with some initial design thoughts. Do not wait until you are building the pages. Start talking mock-ups from the beginning.

INITIAL DESIGNS

Creating a design for the Web is very different than designing a brochure or printed document. XploreNet worked with the BMG Web committee to come up with some initial design thoughts. This included the main page design, also known as the graphic interface. XploreNet worked with BMG to make sure the new design gave the user control over the experience. Modern Web users expect a level of design sophistication from all Web pages. The goal is to provide for the needs of the target users, adapting the technology to the user's expectations. Never frustrate users by designing roadblocks. The main page's purpose is to aid the user in performing a variety of tasks.

Initial design thoughts are based on the home page or, main page, of the site or application. The main page acts as a common sense entry point. However, keep in mind that some users will enter into the site at sub-page levels. For example, BMG would have visitors coming from search engines, banner ads on industry sites, and seminar material. These outlets would in many cases, offer different landing pages, other than the main page.

The main page is roughly 28 square inches. The top of the page comprises the key real estate on the main page. Most users will immediately look to this part of the site, especially since many users still view pages in a 600 x 800 monitor setting. Therefore, positioning is critical. Similar to a newspaper, stories at the top of the page are read more than those on the bottom. Utilize the top of your main page for the navigation bar and key messages.

Initial design strategies for the main page fall into three main categories:

Channel-based main pages
▸▸ This main page strategy is typically utilized by firms with large sites, offering so much information to several different user groups that putting all the appropriate links and content on the main page would cause the page to be overwhelming to all visitors. Furthermore, users visit these types of sites for specific information or tasks. If your site is this large, then it would likely make sense to divide it into different categories and offer more details in specific sections. For example, you might have three key divisions in a company. The menu options might be Asia, North American, and South America.

Menu-driven main pages
▸▸ In the early days of the Internet, and even now, text based links dominate main pages. This type of design is dominated by plain lists of text based HTML hyperlinks. More complicated designs combine blocks of text links and graphic links. Typically text links are much easier to edit while graphic links are more space efficient.

News or information main pages
▸▸ This type of design strategy is used by non-profits organizations that sell nothing or news organizations (USA Today, CNN, etc.). These firms utilize their main page to make announcements on what's new or the day's main news stories. This is information that is updated daily or hourly, thus the site is more likely to experience repeat visitors. Most firms utilize their main page for event updates or late-breaking news. In order to utilize this strategy to its full effect, make sure the location of the news or updated

information stays consistent. If you make changes or revisions often, keep this information in the same place.

BMG chose to work with a menu-driven design. The company came to this decision because after going through the Analysis Phase and at the beginning of the Blue Print Phase, it was discovered that their calls to action were more appropriate for this type of strategy. As you start to prepare the initial mock-ups, fall back on your user profile. It's difficult to design for all audiences or unknown users whose preferences you know nothing about. BMG matched the users and their scenarios to the design, asking the question, "Would a targeted user, attempting to find specific information or complete our call to action, be hindered by the main page design?" Performing usability testing and getting feedback is the best method by which to determine if your main page gets portrays your message accordingly. There are several critical areas to think about:

Match the main purpose/goals to the design

▸▸ When you begin a project, you must have your priorities already established. What are the most common objectives? You defined them earlier in the goals portion of Module 1. Now it's time to connect the dots.

Focus on the main page or main user interface section

▸▸ This is the foundation of your design—every thing should be built around this primary component. The navigation system, overall look and feel, brand objectives, and calls to action should now be considered. From the main page, you can identify sub pages and required content.

Complete mock-ups of all key user pages

▸▸ Create mock-ups of all pages where a user is given a call to action such as purchase a product, inquire about a service, log in to an account, etc. These pages are simply Photoshop files with minimal HTML or functionality. If done properly, the mock-ups can help reduce time spent rebuilding pages. Do not build out any HTML until the design is agreed upon.

TESTING YOUR IDEAS

Getting opinions on your mock-ups can be a difficult process. Web pages can be like art, one person's treasure is another person's trash. If you have the budget, do a full usability test (which includes five different categories and a set process). If not, perform a simple one. Choose three to four designs that fit most of the goals from Phase 1. Locate four to five users from the defined user groups and test (The next section covers usability testing in detail). Create two to four mock-ups for each test page. Ask questions, have the testers work with the navigation, and establish your calls to action. For example, how would you (the user) contact us? How would you purchase services from us? What content looks appealing or causes curiosity?

AVOID SPLASH SCREENS

A quick note on splash screens or intro pages: while attractive, they should typically be avoided. They serve no good purpose and can annoy the first-time user, and especially, the repeat user. They are often built in Flash, which can take a long time to load or may not load correctly.

BMG realized that the initial designs would set the foundation for the rest of their site. At this point you will make your design decisions based on past user feedback and internal ideas and goals. Although the overall "look and feel" will make the first impression, the organization of the menu and key information will either help the user in the next step or drive the user away. After the usability testing, BMG knew whether they had hit the target or needed to go back to the drawing board.

Usability Testing Defined (2.8)

Purpose:	Understand how your visitors will use the site or Web application via usability testing
Key Points:	You will use your initial design mock-ups to test your ideas. Users will either confirm your theories or show you where you missed the mark. It is critical to be impartial in this phase. For example, you may really love the color orange, but the user doesn't think it matches your objectives. Listen to the feedback and implement what works best for the *user*.

When you look at your favorite Web sites, what about them appeals to you most? What do your Web site's visitors like about yours? It's not uncommon for your different customer/prospect segments to behave differently. Each segment may need different types of information and be drawn to specific parts of your Web site. How do you know your Web site is delivering the information customers and prospects need to buy from you, versus your competition?

For nearly as long as the Internet has become a popular medium, XploreNet has designed Web sites and Web-based technology solutions. And from this vast and diverse experience of serving clients in multiple industries, we've learned the best way to know what your customers and prospects want, **is to** *ask* them.

LACK OF USABILITY TESTING

If you've ever visited a Web site or online tool and felt frustrated, lost or downright disappointed, it is often because of one key element: when the site was built, no usability testing was completed. BMG's current Web site did not have any usability testing conducted before it was launched. They didn't ask their most important group (site visitors) how they felt about the site and other questions, like: Does the navigation make sense? Does the user understand the calls to action? The easiest way to lose a visitor is poor usability.

USABILITY TESTING PROCESS

Understand Web usability by performing the Grandma test. Imagine your Grandma sitting in front of her PC, accomplishing a list of tasks. As she works through the tasks, she provides feedback, rates the difficulty, and the observer makes notes. If a Grandma (in this case, stereotypical of the most basic Web user) can navigate and accomplish the calls to action, then the majority of your audience should be able to do so as well.

XploreNet conducted usability testing with 10 participants for BMG, utilizing the mock-ups created in the initial design sessions. We performed the usability testing procedure outlined in Module 5 in the Web Plan.

The usability process looks like this:

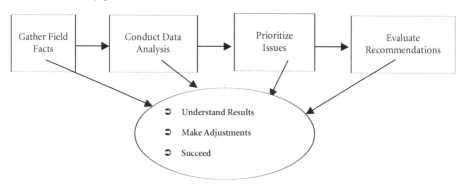

IDENTIFYING PARTICIPANTS

You will need to identify a proper group of participants (beginner to advanced users, as well as a diversity of demographics including men, women, younger to more mature, etc.). The goal is to test users from the site's target audience—complete tasks typical of those they would do "in everyday, real-world scenarios". For example, BMG wanted their users to know how to shop online, how to find the right contact for enterprise software purchases, and how to sign up for the elearning courses they offer. Your testing procedures might ask the user to input user names/passwords, find contact information, and/or purchase or donating something.

All participants have different ability levels—beginner, intermediate, and advanced. Furthermore, make sure participants are asked consistent questions and tasks in the same sequence. The tasks should be divided up into broad-brush tests and priority questions covering a few important elements or calls to action.

TEST QUESTIONS

You should identify 15 to 25 key questions, including a three to five question pre-test designed to gather background information. The pre-test typically includes demographic information such as level of Internet/computer experience, age, company role, gender, type of computer, browser they prefer/use, connection speed to the Internet, etc. During the test, ask participants to accomplish specific tasks (i.e. sign up for something, contact a specific office, etc.), and make sure you understand how the user uses the site. Tabulate the results by setting up the data in a database format or as a simple Excel spreadsheet. Finally, make the appropriate recommendations for the proper design and development based on the data results.

TESTING METHODS

Once you know what questions to ask, decide on the most appropriate testing method. The most common testing methods include:

▶▶ An email survey sent to a specified group—typically 100 to 500 participants.

▶▶ Perform testing via telephone interviews while the subjects view mock-ups and navigation on their computer.

▶▶ Perform testing in a laboratory, where you may record both audio and video results.

All interviews should last between 25 minutes and an hour. For BMG, telephone interviews made the most sense. XploreNet contacted the identified participants and walked them through the process, completing a pretest questionnaire before beginning. The results of the usability testing are not intended to be the sole decision criteria of the final design. Instead, they are a guide.

Combine the data with the other details you uncovered in the Analysis Phase. BMG considered all factors, including the initial designs, usability test results, and overall company objectives to determine which design would work best for their targeted users.

Technical Personnel (2.9)

Purpose:	Understand which technical personnel should be involved and proper timing
Key Points:	In order to know when to bring in the technical staff, you must know both their strengths and weaknesses. The more complex the project is, the earlier the technical staff should be involved. Make sure you have set specific goals for your technical staff.

For a web project to succeed you need to understand the important role the technical personnel will play in the success of the project. Timing and the process you use to engage them is a critical part of your web plan.

WHEN TO GET THE GURUS INVOLVED

You should get your technical gurus involved as soon as possible on most Web-related projects. A technical guru typically approaches the project strictly from the technical side. Often, they do not have a clear understanding, nor are they concerned what occurs in the user interface or the marketing aspects of your Web project. Remain aware that technical gurus rarely think beyond their own technical scope. Therefore, keep your technical gurus in check.

DEALING WITH THE TECHNICAL PERSONALITY

Technical personalities tend to focus on how something will work, observing the proper code and the functional process. They may often overlook things like calls to action, sales process, and content relevance. However, their input is incredibly important. They are often a very effective sounding board or idea testing tool. You may have great ideas on the front end or user side, but that may not be practical when it comes to your resources, budget requirements, timelines, or functional requirements. The technical guru can also help to keep you in check.

BMG made certain their technical personnel involved on the project were given the opportunity to voice their opinions and concerns. Great ideas can be killed by not letting the technical gurus provide feedback and make suggestions. This should include both your internal staff and your outsourced partner. Make them part of the entire solution. Help them to stay on track, listing priorities and technology options, covering timetables and platform options. The more you inform the technical gurus about specific project goals and timelines, the better the interaction of the technical team. In the end this results in a successful project.

Future Plans (2.10)

Purpose:	Understand how your Web project will evolve over the next 12, 24, 36 months
Key Points:	Future Web plans are not like future business plans. Web plans are shorter and must take into consideration ever-evolving, new technologies. However, continue to match business and marketing objectives to your future Web plans.

Planning for the future when covering any business function is difficult, but the process becomes even more difficult when technology is involved. Since we don't have a crystal ball, we have to go with established best practices and take a shot at making lots of assumptions. Some will be correct and many (maybe even most) will probably be wrong.

TECHNOLOGY CYCLES

Technology is ever-changing and doing so rapidly. The latest statistics provide a 12 to 18 month cycle, meaning that new technology is coming every 12 to 18 months and in some cases every six months. This uncertainty made it difficult for BMG to estimate what changes would need to be implemented in the future. However, they understood the importance of establishing how to work with new technology, and the effects on the company's business objectives and rules.

DEVELOPING FUTURE PLANS

Even though it is difficult to predict, you must still plan for the future. How do you do this? First, understand that any Web-related project, whether it is a new Web site or new Web application, is a continually evolving process. BMG's new Web tools were built on the Microsoft .Net platform, which is recommended when future enhancements and growth are anticipated. As your business changes, so will changes be made in the technology required to operate it. Therefore, establish both strategies and tactics. Tactics should define how your new Web strategies will be implemented. BMG's tactics included future personnel needs, the number of reoccurring small projects; add-ons, and special future SalesLogix applications.

When it comes to the Web, you have a large advantage—it is much easier to change than most aspects of a business. Although technology projects can have steep price tags, these are comparable to changing your location. Programs can be rewritten in far less time than it took in the past. New tools can be added on, often in only weeks or months, rather than years.

Future Web plans take into consideration your company's future business environment; staff needs, customer service, production processes, and sales and marketing systems. When you look into the future, try to understand how the new technology will help or hinder these key areas. In the end, you'll have an evolving plan that fits your current business plan and shapes your future business plans.

COMPLETION OF MODULE 2

You have now completed the Blue Print Phase of your Web plan. Refer to Module 5 for the outline and details of a properly constructed Web plan. The Blue Print Phase is critical to the success of your Web strategies and the projects that enable those strategies. After completing modules one and two, the foundation of the Web plan is completed. At this point, BMG knew who, what, how, and when, their Web strategies would be fulfilled. The next step of completing the actual construction of the new Web project can be successfully and efficiently completed.

MODULE 3: CONSTRUCT

3.0 Construct

This module discusses the next phase of understanding how your Web project fit into your Web plan. You will quickly learn how to match the deliverables to an end product. This is where you build out the Web project. Utilizing the information obtained in Phases 1 and 2, you have the right information to begin and complete the construction process successfully.

Consider the similarities between assembling a building and a Web project. The final product is only as good as the engineering strategies and the blue print. In this module, we cover important areas like architecture and navigation, project management processes, project management tools, the communication process, and quality control.

Most books and Web firms cover the construction phase of a Web site strictly from the technical view point. However, the construction phase of any Web project is the implementation of the strategies (Analysis Phase) and the design issues (Blue print Phase). This is where the written details become *real*, enabling your team and the users to see and use the end product. If the first two modules were covered correctly, the construction phase is simplified.

Architecture & Navigation (3.1)

Purpose: Understand how the project blue print will be implemented

___

Key Points: In this section we cover the comparison to building a Web site
                or application and putting up a large high rise building. You

> will make the connection and understand why issues can become complex very quickly. You will understand the importance of having a detailed architecture and simple navigation.

The City of Denver is currently finishing the construction of a new convention center and convention hotel. The construction has taken place over the last year. Each day people see new levels completed, new equipment put in place, and different personnel with different roles. By understanding how a large building is constructed, you'll have a better feel for how a complex Web project is built.

ARCHITECTURE & NAVIGATION

You may be asking yourself how erecting a building relates to a Web project. The answer may be more than you realize. The key is your project's architecture and navigation. Instead of pouring concrete, moving heavy objects in place, putting up walls, and installing electrical and mechanical systems, you're implementing a blue print for success on the Web. It is amazing how architects create blue prints that show construction superintendents and foremen all the right parts, to fit at all the right times, in all the right places. There is a remarkable synergy between buildings and Web sites, and the same elements and processes between architecture and Web development. You can garner some great "tricks of the trade" from the architectural design process that can be applied to building a new Web project.

The challenge with most Web sites is that the developer(s) did not look at the site as an architect would look at a building. In fact, many sites would be condemned if they were buildings. If you could provide all the information on one page, navigation wouldn't matter. The modern Web makes this almost impossible, so you need a quality navigational structure. Sites and tools that require you to click four, five, and six times into the site or have to click back six levels to get to the main page have completely missed the target. If you had a building that required you to figure out how to get to the fifth floor with no signs or elevators, your visitors would be in trouble. Many sites do this to the user and this hurts business.

THE DIFFERENCE BETWEEN ARCHITECTURE AND NAVIGATION

In order to build a great site or Web project with simple navigation, you must understand all the areas we've covered in Phases 1 and 2, as well as understanding the difference between architecture and navigation. The two work hand in hand, but they are unique. Navigation on the Web is defined as the user moving from one page to another within the site; architecture is defined as the design of those pages (both static and dynamic) and the connection between them, to incorporate the navigation system. A good way to think of this difference involves that architecture is the arrangement and make-up of the content, while navigation involves the devices that move the user from one page to another.

USERS PERCEPTION OF NAVIGATION

The user's ability to navigate should be as straightforward and simple as possible. Keep in mind that users will not memorize your navigational structure. "At IBM and at Sun, we studied how people read on the Web. What we discovered is they don't! They scan," says Jakob Nielsen, a distinguished former Sun Microsystems engineer. The user is scanning the pages for key words, phrases, and headings. In fact, place as much detail as possible on each page because cross-referencing Web pages too difficult. Finally make it simple for the user to follow your information in a process—step A, step B, step C, etc.

Some navigation structures are involved, pushing users to certain sections of the site. The problem is that users won't take the time to learn the logic of your navigation. Users want the right information to lead to the right call to action, right now. If the navigation is understated, the user will get lost; if the navigation is overwhelming they'll simply leave (close the browser).

You must create the navigation with a logical process in mind because a high percentage of the visitors to your site will be repeat visitors. Once they've been to your site several times they'll know where to find what they need. However, the navigation should be very obvious to the new visitor, as well. Simple navigation enables the new visitor to find what they need quickly.

EDUCATING THE USER

No matter how visitors get to your site or Web application, chances are they are going to be unfamiliar with it. If they get to the site via a search engine then the process gets even more difficult. They may be dumped into a section other than that of your main page even a back page, that is not regularly. Therefore, it is important to make sure that main menu and key links are very apparent.

Here are some strategies to help your visitors navigate through your site when they come from a search engine.

▸▸ Craft a clear message about the purpose of the site

▸▸ Usability is your key

▸▸ Define useful and simple navigation

▸▸ Include critical information that the user expects

▸▸ Develop beneficial content

GREAT NAVIGATION

Great navigation is about simplicity and common sense. How do you create an environment that facilitates users to navigate your Web project correctly? One important element of navigation is called top-level navigation, and consists of the main page of the application or main page of the site. In addition, pay close attention to the main navigation structure or main menu choices. As most people know, this is either the menu across the top or down the left hand side of the page. Now, what makes sense to the user (review back to usability for more details)?

Architecture and navigation work hand in hand on the Web, assisting the user to get what they want. That is the real measure of successful architecture and navigation. Did the user find what he was searching for? Simple navigation works and typically costs less to build and maintain.

Project Management Process (3.2)

Purpose:	Evaluate the proper process to implement your scope of work
Key Points:	In this section we'll cover a potential project process. If you follow an established process, you're more likely to implement a successful solution.

Project management is one of the most important components of completing a new Web project and is often the component most overlooked. A full life cycle project management process is the vital link that holds every development project together. In fact, you must have buy-in from your top executives and a plan in place to accomplish the following: defined project plan, schedule, resources, budget, risks, and scope. The key elements to a successful project are validation, organization, initiation, management, and completion. When you approach a redesign or the development of a complex tool for the Web, you must understand how the process will work. A well organized, simple process will increase your success rate, while a lack on one very likely results in failure.

PROJECT MANAGEMENT OVERVIEW

The field of project management has been studied in great detail, yet many of the processes are difficult for people to grasp and articulate. Since 2000, the number of studies related to project management has increased significantly. The results are still mixed. According to CIO Insight, CIOs are knee-deep in IT projects these days. But when it comes to managing these initiatives, companies often lack discipline, thanks to half-hearted involvement and insufficient follow-up. Here are some statistics provide by CIO Insight:

▸▸ 53 percent of CIOs say their IT project prioritization is politically driven

▸▸ 40 percent of CIOs use a portfolio management approach to IT projects

▸▸ 66 percent of IT projects during the past 12 months came in at or below budget

▸▸ 13 percent of IT projects failed to meet the goals of IT and business management

THE PROCESS

Many firms forget that completing a usable, successful site requires a process. Often, they, or rather, their clients, are disappointed with the end result, blaming the mistakes on poor design, when the reality is they did not utilize the right process. Their project management process was incomplete or non-existent, causing delays, misunderstandings, and frustration.

The project management process is not about completing an initial planning meeting and then going to work. It's about daily or weekly updates, identifying what works and what doesn't. You'll need to initially validate the new project (covered in Module 1). Then, get organized and relax, knowing how all the pieces will fit together. Get started and never look back. Analysis can become paralysis very quickly. Furthermore, commit to ongoing management whether the project takes six weeks or one year, or more. The best part is always the completion point. You'll be done before you know it. In addition, using the scope of work as the blue print, draw a flowchart for the process. If you're working with a development company, they should have a process for you to utilize. If you're on your own, refer to the XploreNet Web plan at the end of this book or email info@xplorenet.com to receive information on the proper process.

The process should look like this:

Understanding the details of this process will allow the delivery of successful results. There are many key issues including planning, implementation and quality control. There are also challenges in every step, which will need to be overcome. You may have several people involved with different goals and agendas. The challenge of understanding who does what and when can be overwhelming. Several key areas are involved the process:

▸▸ Identify who the lead person or persons are

▸▸ The method for completing each step and getting to the next one

▸▸ Define who is responsible for what

▸▸ Establish Realistic timelines

▸▸ Key questions and answers

Create a task check-list from the deliverables, using the following tips:

▸▸ Find somewhere quiet, with no interruptions, to complete the check-list

▸▸ Create check-lists at the start of the project, near the middle, and at the end

▸▸ Print out a rough draft list, adding notes as you go along

▸▸ Review each task on the list, go away, come back, and either confirm or delete it

▸▸ Identify which tasks will cause the biggest challenges

▸▸ Make sure the entire team understands all tasks

PROJECT MANAGER

A good project manager is critical for a successful project. This includes both the person in charge of your Web project at your firm and at your outsourced vendor. The project manager has several goals, but one focus: finish the project on time and within budget. They need to be able to handle administrative tasks, the people involved, and the details of the Web plan—all simultaneously. This means the project manager's main skills are to communicate effectively and to multitask. He also must be accountable for the entire project. Accountability on most projects is often overlooked. This means defining who is responsible, and for what. Make sure you have it clearly detailed in the plan as to who is not only responsible for what task, but who is responsible for the strategic initiatives and tactical implementation.

TIMELINES

Make sure timelines are clearly defined and understood by the entire team. Ask the key question, "Are our timelines realistic?" Have a back up plan for challenges that arise during the project. Change and challenges always come up, so don't be stress when they appear—be prepared for them ahead of time. Have a detailed process, often called change/challenge management for handling the scope and technology changes. New ideas and better methods can emerge. So don't kill them. Instead, have a process to facilitate them.

A correct project management process will help all the players understand their roles. Furthermore, the process will help monitor project activities and deliverables against the plan. It should help with tracking challenges, communicating progress, and identifying the successes and failures learned for the next project.

Project Management Tools (3.3)

Purpose:	Evaluate the proper project tools to implement the scope of work
Key Points:	Understand the types of tools and view an example of the proper project management tool. You should know what categories to cover and how the tool(s) help both the internal team and the outsourced vendor.

Once you have a properly aligned project process, you must have the tools to accomplish your most important initiatives at the right time. There are a million choices when it comes to project management tools. We do not make specific recommendations, but rather provide some general guidelines and helpful hints of what the chosen tool should contain, at the minimum level. As you read through the options you'll begin to see how matching your needs to the tools makes the choice for your Web project clear.

Utilizing a tool that fits your needs provides many benefits. If you've used a project management tool in the past you'll see what might have been missing and if you've never used a Web-based tool, your life is about to get a little easier.

PROJECT MANAGEMENT TOOLS

Project management tools come in many forms and you may even have an internal project management tool in existence. Here are a few "best practices" for a project management tool. Make sure any system you use has at least the following components:

Security

▸ The tool should be secure and only allow access via a user name and password. It is most productive to have a unique username for each member of the project.

Web-based, 24/7 access

▸ The tool should be on the Web, accessible 24 hours a day, seven days a week and not require any special software downloads or plug ins.

Scope of Work

▸ The tool should have a link to the scope of work to enable all involved in the project to see how the work has been defined.

Task List & Task Tracking

▸ The tool should enable both you and your outsourced vendor to update and add to the task list and have a built-in task tracking system. The system should monitor tasks assigned to individual team members and alert both internal and external team members when a task has been missed or changed. This prevents a small problem from becoming a large one.

Automated Emailing

▸ The tool should have the capability of an automated "'elective emailing system" that performs peripheral tasks such as sending appropriate emails to project team members, whenever required. This ensures you are free to concentrate on the core project-management functions.

Upload Area

▸ This area can be utilized by either the internal or external personnel to FTP content, text, graphics, links, etc. to the project management tool.

Document Sharing

▸ Make sure all team members can upload files and documents related to the project. The files and documents section should contain all the project-related files and documents that personnel may have posted for the review process.

Discussion Board/Communication Center

▸ Utilizing a threaded discussion area improves communication between internal team members and the outsourced vendor drastically; it also aims to eliminate communication gaps that exist within teams and in the correspondence with clients and other external agencies. One way to accomplish this is to enable team members to post their views and questions, to be answered or commented upon by other members. You may see the discussions for all tasks or see them listed separately.

Project Reporting

▸▸ You should be able to download or receive project reports for all aspects of the project. The reports should reflect overall project summary, the tasks that are pending or completed, the contact information for each team member, and the discussion threads or project updates.

BENEFITS

The benefits of utilizing the proper tool during a Web-related project are immense. In fact, if you do not use this type of tool you may be handicapping the project right from the beginning. Here are a few of the benefits of utilizing a project management tool

▸▸ Enhanced communication between team members

▸▸ Hitting milestones successfully and on time

▸▸ Better project team management

▸▸ Cost effectiveness

▸▸ Quality completed project

Utilizing the right project management tools improves operational competencies, leading to real ROI. Companies are continually searching for ways to do more with less. All project tools should be viewed strictly by how they improve the final product. The correct tools will save every member of your staff time, and enable your next project to meet the expectations set out in the beginning.

Development Process (3.4)

Purpose:	Understand the proper process for developing Web projects
Key Points:	Evaluate the proper development process and implement the steps where necessary.

Every new Web project poses challenges, but having a well-defined development process can help. In section 3.2 we covered the project management process. In this section we get into specifics of the development process. If you complete Web projects in-house, make sure you incorporate some of the following ideas into your plan. And if you use an outsourced vendor, make sure they have an existing process.

DEVELOPMENT PROCESS

Developing a large Web project is a process that may affect your business in several ways, including budgetary choices, personnel utilized, and sales results. One problem is that too many new Web projects begin as off the cuff, disorganized messes. The projects are often started by small groups within organizations, working in isolation to accomplish their own agendas. The results can be devastating.

The process should include a step-by-step approach, anticipating problems. The process should be clear and simple, so that all involved understand how the actual pages will be completed.

A typical development process looks like the following:

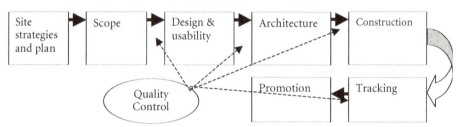

As you consider the development process outlined above, note that the construction of the pages that make up the Web site is one of the last things that takes place in a well-designed project. Consider each step in the process and its impact on your specification plan. Think before you act, and make sure you have the organizational backing, budget, and personnel resources you'll need to make the project a success.

Communication Process (3.5)

Purpose:	Understand the process for communicating during a project and overcoming expected obstacles
Key Points:	In this section you will learn what can hamper the communication process during a Web project. You will understand what to expect and how to overcome the obstacles so that you end up with an open and productive communication process.

Communication has a big impact on projects, from start to finish. The human art of communication takes on an amazingly difficult step during Web projects. There are many reasons why it is difficult. Common mistakes can be overcome easily and simply when your follow a well-designed communication process.

There are many factors that we covered in the project management process that will help, however, what can be used during the project to make the process better? Furthermore, how can a process help make the completion of your new Web project successful?

THE PROCESS

Web projects involve many parts working together properly. Can you imagine trying to complete all the different parts of the project with no communication?

You must utilize a process that involves initial ground rules. At the very first meeting discuss how the communication will take place and by whom. Identify how often, and what will be done if the communication breaks down. Ensure that each team member understands each other's ideas, issues, and challenges. As the project moves forward, different problems will arise.

Here is a potential process:

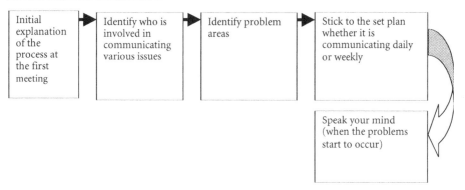

No process is wrong, but the key is to have the process in place. Articulate it to all involved in the project. This way you get away from the assumptions (we all know what assumptions do).

Build Pages (3.6)

Purpose:	Understand when to build out the pages
Key Points:	In this section, we cover the proper time to build the actual web pages

It probably seems strange to talk about building Web pages in the third phase of a development project. Besides, isn't building the Web pages the main point of any Web project? Building the pages is the easiest part of any Web project. The standard technology is the same whether you use HTML, DHTML, Flash, XML, etc.—the code is simply code. What matters, is the personnel implementing the code and their ability to insert the code without error.

THE TIME IS RIGHT

Now that you've completed roughly 36 parts to your Web plan, you're ready to build the pages. In fact, if you've done the previous phases correctly, this part of your project is the most straight-forward. There is nothing left to do, but have your team build out the pages. However, make sure you monitor the process with established quality control practices and that the personnel building the pages have the right direction and ability to finish the Web project without errors and within budget and time constraints.

Quality Control & Testing (3.7)

Purpose:	Understand the process for quality control
Key Points:	In this section you will learn a process for controlling the quality of your end product. Evaluate different options for testing procedures.

When applied to Web projects the term quality control describes working to improve the quality control process. Indeed, you must understand and enforce the quality control standards and processes used to produce the end product. This includes its technical components, architecture, and content. If you have the right quality control process in place, a new Web site should see a decrease in bugs (defective programming) and an improvement in site usability and performance.

HOW TO IMPLEMENT

Quality control should enhance the user's experience, helping the developers to design a site or application with the users in mind. Brainstorm on all the factors that can go wrong—what will we need to overcome, other than the traditional problems?

Focus on understanding and tracking the problems. Proper quality control for a Web project involves an interaction with the internal development team and outsourced vendor, at several levels, in order to find bugs and provide clarification. The process should catch and report problems and direct the issues to the right person for resolution. The test is simple. The code passes or fails, and is then referred to the team to identify who is responsible and figure out how it will be fixed. Test again and then solve until completion.

A properly established quality control process contains a reporting typically Web based and track able. The system should enable the development team to recognize problems, report them via the Web, and track their resolution. Make sure you have a clear understanding of how the problems will be dealt with, who will be responsible for what, and the expectations regarding the timeline on getting the problem fixed.

QUALITY CONTROL CHECK LIST

Before the final site or application is launched live make sure you test for the following:

▸▸ Compatibility with the hosting platform

▸▸ Database issues

▸▸ Bugs in the code

▸▸ Download speeds from 56K and up

▸▸ Spelling and grammar

▸▸ User Interface usability

▸▸ FTP access

▸▸ Administration areas (do usernames and passwords work)

▸▸ Security issues

Launching a new Web project with out completing the proper quality control and testing procedures can cause embarrassment and in some situations, the loss of employment. In the end, make sure all deliverables have been accomplished and everything works properly before the new site or application goes live.

COMPLETION OF MODULE 3

You have now completed the Construction phase of your Web plan. Refer to Module 5 for the outline and details of a properly constructed Web plan. The construction phrase is simple if Phases One and Two were completed. However, make sure that the personnel, whether internal or external, have the capabilities and drive to finish the project with out error and on time. After completing Modules 1, 2, and 3, your new Web project is complete, meaning the actual pages are built and the site or application is live. Next, we'll help you match the online marketing tools to the objectives you established in Module 1.

MODULE 4: DRIVE

4.0 Drive

This module discusses the next phase of understanding in the life cycle of your Web presence or Web tools. At this point you have a new Web project built that meets your company objectives, matches your brand, and facilitates interaction. You're finished right? Not quite. The old saying, "build it and they will come" just doesn't hold true any more. No matter whether the new site is provided for internal use or for prospective customers, promoting the usage is a large component to the success or failure of the site or new application. You will quickly understand how to match Web-based promotional tools to your overall business objectives. This is critical to the success of your project. The ideas and tools for promotion are a large part of your overall Web plan.

The Internet has fast become a mainstream communications medium and businesses ranging from start up to Fortune 100 are forced to promote their Web presences. Understanding how to drive traffic to your redesigned Web project is an ongoing process. Don't look for short cuts; they don't exist. You will need to take a long-term approach to all your promotional strategies.

Most books and Web firms cover a promotional phase strictly from the tactical view point (search engines, email, and traditional marketing). We cover those important areas, but jump more into the marketing initiatives or the 'why' behind the tactical issues. We help you connect Module 1, where you covered business and marketing goals, to the actual implementation.

Start at the End (4.1)

Purpose:	Understand how the promotional tools fit into the overall marketing objectives

Key Points:	In this section you will learn a process for evaluating and implementing the correct Web-based promotional tools. Just because it exists, does not mean you should use it. You will understand how to set budgets, evaluate options, and make adjustments.

In Phase 1, we discussed goals and users. Part of developing the marketing goals in Module 1 was to match each goal to an online marketing tool. Now you can evaluate which tools will help you accomplish the most important business and sales goals. If the goal is to increase traffic, search engines and are the initial match. If one of the goals was to increase existing client usage or repeat visitors, then traditional methods or improved content, are important. For example, postcards, letters, and messages with specific promotions or opportunities should point the client or visitor to a certain section of the site.

START AT THE END

You must start with the end in mind. In the initial Analysis Phase we covered how some of the promotional tools can help make business results obtainable. Part of establishing the ROI is to understand how all your marketing tools will work together. The number one step is to evaluate both traditional (direct mail, ads, TV, newspaper, etc.) and digital (search engines, banner ads, email, etc.) will work together. There are plenty of books on traditional marketing tools so we will not get in-depth here. However, when it comes to digital tools the key is to match the tools to the objective.

For now don't worry about the actual tools and how they'll be implemented. We need to focus on initial plans and objectives. If you're going to use search engines, then make sure that during the design process, the pages are optimized for the engines. Also, if you will use email promotions or newsletters, make sure there is a process on the site to take people from the email to the site. In the end, this module will assist you in laying the groundwork for a detailed, online marketing and sales strategy that matches your goals.

Online Marketing Strategy (4.2)

Purpose:	Understand all the parts of an online marketing strategy and how to correctly implement the tools
Key Points:	In this section you will learn a process for evaluating and implementing the correct online marketing strategies. You will understand how to establish the strategies and complete the tactics, matching the options to the overall marketing objectives.

Just getting a new project off the ground can be time consuming and overwhelming. In fact, finding the time to complete a critical step in the process, such as completing the specifics of your online strategies, can be difficult. There are so many other moving parts to the redesign or building process that it is tempting to simply overlook the details of this part of your plan. However, if you put the time into this phase, you'll reap the rewards in the end.

DEFINITION

A detailed online marketing strategy is like a GPS system to a car, enabling you to get to the exact targeted destination. As opportunities present themselves, or your competitive environment takes on a new look, the tactics within the overall strategy can be modified or enhanced. The strategies will point you in the best direction for all your decisions.

The online marketing strategies should be part of your overall business and marketing objectives. As we mentioned in Phase One, you'll need to match each tool to the correct metrics. In fact, it is critical for you to align each tool to the specific goals you defined in Phase 1.

The reality is a great looking site, with none of the online marketing strategies becoming useless in the end. According to Forrester Research, "72% of new Web sites do not meet the criteria of being a marketable tool." How do you fit into the 28 percent that meet the criteria? Online Web strategies encompass the following categories:

▶▶ Ecommerce tools

▶▶ Email

▶▶ Search engine marketing—directories and engines

▶▶ Affiliate marketing

▶▶ Strategic alliances

➧ Traditional marketing tools

➧ Customer tools

➧ Innovative ideas

The key to a proper online Web strategy is a balance of all the available tools, and matching each tool to an ROI indicator.

Ecommerce Strategies (4.3)

Purpose:	Understand how to effectively implement ecommerce tools on your site and properly promote the products

Key Points:	In this section you will learn how to implement an ecommerce strategy. We cover the potential tools, the shopping process, and the strategies to drive traffic.

Ecommerce has transformed the Web over the last 10 years from a brochure tool to a viable way to reach revenue and profit goals. According to Webopedia, the definition of ecommerce or, *electronic commerce,* is business that is conducted over the Internet, using any of the applications that rely on the Internet, such as email, instant messaging, shopping carts, Web services, UDDI, FTP, and EDI, and others. Electronic commerce can occur between two businesses (B2B) transmitting funds, goods, services and/or data, or between a business and a customer (B2C). For our purposes we're tackling ecommerce strictly for the selling of goods, where a financial transaction takes place in real time on the Web. In order to implement the right tools and strategy, you must understand the market opportunity, the tools, merchant accounts, and promotional methods.

STATISTICS

In 2004, Forrester Research predicted North America to realize USD 3.5 trillion in ecommerce transactions, while the Asia-Pacific can expect USD 1.6 trillion, and Europe should see USD 1.5 trillion. The market is good and only getting better for ecommerce. You may already be taking advantage of this opportunity or you may be starting to investigate it.

IMPLEMENTING AN ECOMMERCE STRATEGY

The first step in implementing an ecommerce program is to identify which products you will sell. For our purposes we're covering products that can be bought online and then, either downloaded or shipped to the customer. Next, you'll need to review the shopping process options. This is usually referred to as the shopping cart. How do you pick the right option?

Choosing an online shopping cart that fits your needs is a critical decision. Similar to a brick and mortar retail establishment, the shopping process on your Web site is your only opportunity to impress potential buyers. If the shopping process is hectic and difficult, a retail store can go out of business, very quickly. This is true for your Web site's shopping cart, as well. If the user has problems, he's gone. In fact, the most important part of the shopping cart is the customer's private information and credit card numbers. If you do not deal with this information in the right method, you'll lose sales. Security is paramount.

There are several options when it comes to shopping carts. They range from Web-based systems where your site simply links to the cart, or on-site systems that require programming to integrate the cart into the site. The three main categories include merchant services like eBay, hosted shopping carts, and integrated shopping carts.

Merchant shopping carts like eBay require you to utilize your own merchant account and gateway. A merchant account is the bank account that enables your site to take credit cards, while the gateway enables the transaction to be completed over a secure Internet connection. A site like eBay will allow you to use their system (merchant account and gateway), but you pay higher fees. A merchant service is perfect for companies that are just starting their business or do not have a significant amount of transactions.

Hosted shopping carts are similar to a merchant system except they include the merchant account, gateway, and shopping cart. They typically charge an upfront set-up fee and then a small fee for each transaction. This is also good for a small business just starting out. The negatives of this choice include a templated cart (your image may not match their offerings) and few functional options other than the base plan.

An integrated shopping cart is a full custom, programmed cart. You receive all the "bells and whistles" and can often leverage many different technologies to up-sell or cross-sell various items. This process is the best option; however, it will be the most costly.

Once you've chosen the best option for your ecommerce process, you will need to run tests with usability (How easy is the cart to use?), marketing tools (How do you get the user to the cart?), and up-sell or cross-sell opportunities (How do you set up accounts and when do you offer more options?)

COMPLETING THE SALE

Now that you've chosen your options, how do you make sure users complete the sale? Here are some helpful tips:

▶▶ Make the shopping experience simple:
Make sure the products are easy to locate, that pictures and graphics match the product, and that product descriptions are easy to read.

▶▶ Provide detailed explanations:
Explain both your shopping process and other policies in detail. Show a diagram and explain in words, how the person can, and will, shop your site. The more specific your directions are, the more shoppers you will retain.

▶▶ Common sense check out:
Allow the customer to purchase products and/or fill up their shopping cart and then ask for payment. During the payment process, ask for detailed information about the customer. Don't ask for this information before they enter their credit card number and don't over do the questions on the detailed information. Their dog's favorite toy might not be appropriate— stick to the basics—contact information and customer feedback.

▶▶ Multiple shipping options:
Use a shipping company that has on-line order tracking. Make it easy for your customers to use this.

▶▶ Dividing sections:
Make sure your products are divided into categories that make sense. For example, you will want all the wood products to be together, and separate from the metal products, or your consulting services to be separate from your financial services.

▶▶ Accept credit cards:
The great advantage of on-line shopping is its immediacy. The entire transaction should be completed in just a few minutes. Customers will simply leave and go elsewhere where the need for instant completion of the transaction can be fulfilled if your process takes too long, or in the extra time they have before completing the transaction customers may change their minds about purchasing form you. Also, remember that credit cards are by far the easiest way for non-U.S. customers to order directly from the U.S.

▸▸ Confirm Orders:
Make sure the customer not only receives a page saying, "Your order has been received" (or something similar), but also the ability to print out a receipt for their records and receive a confirmation email.

▸▸ Provide Help Areas:
Create a help area similar to FAQ (frequently asked questions). This area should include the FAQs along with methods to get in touch with you, and a link to your live chat tool, if you have one. Address problems that may come up and solve them online whenever possible.

▸▸ List Important Information:
Your customers should be able to place an order without a hassle. Make sure they don't have to fill out three pages of forms before the order is accepted. Receive important information for your database, like name, address, preferences, zip code, etc. *after* they have placed their order. The fewer steps and shorter the process, the more likely the customer is to complete the sale.

▸▸ Remember International Customers
Don't lose orders by narrowing your market just to your home country. Make sure your order form takes international zip codes and provides a valid payment processes. Many sites reject orders if the zip code is not a valid U.S. zip code. International customers have money just like Americans. Many will find your site on a search engine and if your interface is "internationally friendly" they may order. At least give them the option.

IMPROVING THE PROCESS

The key to a well-defined ecommerce strategy is understanding what can go right and wrong in the process. Here are some ideas for improving the process:

▸▸ Anticipate problems:
Your first step in implementing online transactions is to brainstorm on all the challenges. Every online transaction process has problems. The key is to understand each one and either find a solution or create a process for handling the problem. For example, what happens if the credit card number is entered with 17 digits? Does the site crash? Or, is there an explanation page that pops up to direct the user back to the problem field?

▸▸ Shopping cart vs. order form:
Many Web site owners and managers are unsure of when to use a shopping cart tool or build a catalog, and when to use a simple order form. There are two keys to this decision: the number of products in the offering, and the

number of products purchased by each customer during the purchase process. For example, analyze whether your customer will buy just a hat or purchase a pair of socks with shoes and shoe polish. Typically if you have less than 20 products an order form works well. If your customer orders more than two items at one time, a shopping cart mechanism will work best.

▶▶ Dynamic shopping cart:
If you have a lot of products, or make changes frequently, then you will need to use dynamically generated pages. However, many search engines may not index. Design issues come into play with this type of cart in order to offer a seamless appearance to your site.

▶▶ Static shopping cart:
A small amount of code is added to the pages containing your products. This type of cart is great for optimizing each page for the search engines. You will need a maintenance agreement with your development firm when you choose a static cart, and a new page must be created each time you add a new product.

▶▶ Understand the payment process:
Merchant accounts range from no set-up/no monthly fee (but high per-transaction charges) to high set-up/low monthly fee (but relatively low per-transaction charges). The kind of account you choose should depend on how many orders you expect and what of professionalism your visitors expect. Be careful of merchant services that have your visitors leave your Web site to complete their transaction. This customer data is often sold. If you expect a lot of transactions, you'll probably want a merchant account with a bank, offering the bank's own payment process/tool. This assures merchant account/payment processes will be compatible. Don't be conned into signing up for a low-cost Web-store that commits you to high cost, or restrictive, payment processing.

▶▶ Commitment to Privacy:
All the transactions on your site should be protected and secure. All your customers' personal information should be protected and never sold, unless prior permission is given by the customer.

▶▶ Site Performance:
You don't want a sluggish site. Before signing-up check out some reference sites to see how they perform. Remember to test out your Web site and ordering process at different connection speeds, different screen resolutions, and with all the commonly used Web browsers.

▸▸ Resolve problems immediately:
   Your customers must have access to fair, timely, and affordable methods.
   To resolve transaction problems, clear and sufficient information should
   be provided so consumers can make an informed choice. Vendors should
   take reasonable steps to ensure the consumer's choice is informed and
   intentional.

▸▸ Outsource transactions:
   Unless you have very particular server-side requirements, consider very
   carefully before deciding to use your own server, rather than a hosted solution. If you have many hundreds or thousands of items to sell, you should
   really be looking at solutions which link in to a back-end database (or at
   least have an import facility).

▸▸ Timing:
   Get the order to the customer ASAP. The Web is about seconds. Not days.
   Larger competitors will offer free shipping, often with same day delivery,
   while smaller competitors will offer more unique choices. Make sure your
   delivery system and the timing of getting the product/service to the customer is at the same level of quality as the product and customer service.

   The ecommerce strategies that you decide to move forward with will
involve many parts of your business, both technical and process. The information overload can cause headaches. However, you can succeed if you divide the
process into three to four sections and match your overall business strategies
to the specific ecommerce tools.

Online Sales Strategies (4.4)

Purpose:	Understand the choices and possible implementation of the proper online sales strategies

Key Points:	In this section you will learn the various options for online sales tools. You feel confident in implementing specific tools because you will have defined the strategies, understood the limitations, and qualified the budget and resource requirements.

   Virtually every executive or business owner has an image and competitive
anxiety that increased revenue and sales on the Web is just another tool.
However, this tool has become more critical then ever before. You can do so
much more on the Web than you could even as little as six years ago. High
speed access, like DSL and cable, enables users to view video and other

dynamic content in a quick, high quality manner. So how do you develop an online sales strategy that works?

There are several key steps to the process:
- Prioritize your objectives
- Understand the Web sales process
- Evaluate all the tools
- Establish metrics
- Implement for today and the future

IDENTIFY SALES OBJECTIVES

Earlier, in Module 2 Blue Print we covered calls to action. In this section we review the details of the action steps by matching sales objectives to the Web. When you prioritize your objectives you understand to whom you are trying to sell, what you want to sell, and how you want the purchase transaction to be completed.

IMPLEMENTING WEB-BASED TOOLS

Selling on the Web is very different from selling face-to-face. The proper tools and processes to sell from a Web site are often overlooked while developing a new Web project. The difficulties range from not being able to read body language to the inability to ask direct questions. However, you can establish the process, peak interest, and push items directly to the user. Make sure you hit as many senses as possible. Here are some helpful tips:

▶▶ Provide Web presentations:
Use self-paced Web presentations to increase new customer sales through a "real" 24-hour/7-day a week, online store. Your prospective customer can go through a presentation at his own pace and ask specific questions regarding different parts of your product or service.

▶▶ Help your sales reps:
Sales reps are more effective using the Web as a presentation tool and you can reduce appointment costs by having your reps do fulfillment over the phone, using the Web for visual impact. PowerPoint screen shots can be Web enabled and make a lasting impression.

▶▶ Utilize 3rd party tools:
Utilize 3rd party Web tools like Webex.com, evoke.com, etc. to improve Web sales. These sites help users do real-time presentations, combined with conference calls and online chat meetings.

▶▶ Create a special programs section:
Offer special programs in the sales section of your site like buyer clubs; give aways, coupons, prizes, awards, etc. These windows should pop up or link directly from the sales section of your site. If your traffic reporting software allows, show different offers to different prospects, depending on individual profiles.

▶▶ Optimize sales literature:
Save on costly printing and mailing costs by directing requests for product or service information to your Web site. Create brochures, product literature, service benefits and other sales documents in PDF (Adobe's portable document format). Make sure the content is clear and of high quality.

▶▶ Display products properly:
Try not to exceed 30-40K for the total product photo graphics load on a single page. If you need a larger photo size to see detail, make sure a "clickable" thumbnail is incorporated into the design. The thumbnail concept gives the customer the option to view the larger size for more detail. Detailed, quality product photos take up large amounts of disk space. Make sure your hosting company has the space for you. If they set your site up with 50 MB (megabytes) then make sure all MBs are accounted for. Lack of disc space will kill great photos and downloadable video clips quicker than bad design. If the photos and graphics don't load quickly enough, because they're too heavy or because you don't have enough disk space, you'll lose customers—guaranteed.

▶▶ Utilize audio/video:
Include customer testimonials and usage demos in audio and video format in the sales and or product section of your Web site. You can create downloadable or streaming audio or video (make sure you offer multiple choices to your prospects, depending on their Internet connection).

▶▶ Offer email alerts:
Allow customers to sign up for email alerts regarding new products/services. These alerts should offer value as well as pitch. And, that's one more interested customer for your database.

▶▶ Use a sales rep finder:
Many companies forget to offer the biographies of their sales personnel. This information, along with how to contact the sales representative, should be easily

found. Let the prospect or customer know who sells what product or service and the best method to contact that representative.

▸▸ Develop a chat tool for sales representatives:
Enable prospective customers to chat with your sales personnel, either through a live chat tool or a discussion board. Prospects can post questions and sales representatives can answer them at any time of the day, including weekends and holidays.

▸▸ Build a sales FAQ area:
Create an area on your site for frequently asked questions, related to sales, which is updated automatically. For example, if a prospective client asks how many colors item 334 comes the question and the response can be automatically updated to the FAQ area. Therefore, when the next prospect hits the site that specific question and answer are already in the FAQ area. Your sales team members will look like heroes.

The challenge with selling from a Web site is that the prospect is in control, rather than the sales representative. It's the prospect that determines what is seen and when it is seen. However, you can increase your close ratio by offering innovative tools that help the visitor get the information required. In this way, you can still interact with the prospect to accomplish your sales goals.

Search Marketing (4.5)

Purpose:	Understand how the promotional tools fit into overall marketing objectives
Key Points:	In this section you will learn a process for evaluating and implementing the correct Web-based promotional tools. Just because it exists does not mean you should use it. You will understand how to set budgets, evaluate options, and make adjustments.

Search engine marketing or search marketing incorporates the pay-per-click model, optimized pages, and specific seeding on relevant sites. Other terms may be used to describe this process including SEO, SMO, etc. Most people learned of the tremendous power of search marketing via the Google public offering. Google has taken the pay-per-click model to new heights. In this section we'll cover the different portions of search marketing: pay-per-click, page optimization, and positioning.

PAY-PER-CLICK

Pay-per-click search engines, such as Google, Overture, FindWhat.com and 7Search.com, are search sites that return the results of a search based on how much the advertiser bid for placement. The pay-per-click customer sets the budget restraints and the key words to be used, and users click away. The pay-per-click search engine customer that bids the most gets its offering to appear first in the results list; the second-highest appears second, and so on. After all paid advertisers are displayed; all the other results appear just like a regular search engine. If a user clicks on a paid advertiser's offering to go to its Web site, the pay-per-click search engine charges the advertiser's account for the bid amount. Though Google is not actually a pay—per-click search engine, Google does receive the most coverage of any search engine. Google provides what most experts consider the best search results through its sophisticated AdWords marketing campaign.

Typically, Web site owners utilize a pay-per-click provider, either directly or through a Web firm, that manages the click process. The click through rates vary according to how competitive your words are—for example, the per-click rate for "computers" might be $10.00 per click, while the rate for the words "Asian tap dancing" might be .05. One of the newest tools is the Google AdWord tool. When utilizing the AdWord tool, you will typically be able to do a keyword match, which shows your ad when a search includes your selected words and phrase matching, or includes your selected phrases. In addition, an exact query match shows your ad when a search contains your exact key words and no others, while a negative keyword match will not show your ad if a search contains words you select.

OPTIMIZATION

Search engine optimization is the process of creating new pages and optimizing existing pages in order to show up in the organic (natural, non-sponsored) listings of most search engines. Optimized pages can make or break any site that is struggling to define a Web brand. Optimizing Web pages is a topic that comes up every day—to do it, or not. First of all what are optimized pages? This is a page that has been manufactured for the best results in a directory or search engine and includes content, key words, descriptions, and links.

Your Web site may look ecstatically appealing, but search engine directories/spiders don't care about the design. Search engines want a well-organized and well-connected Web site with rich content and informative descriptions of each page. Let's review some of the issues you need to understand to optimize Web pages and Web tools correctly. Remember the following:

Correct and detailed
▸▸ A Meta tag is an element of HTML that often describes the contents of a Web page, and is placed near the beginning of the page's source code. Search engines use information provided in a Meta tags to index pages by subject. Make sure your key words fit your strategy.

Descriptive title tag unique to that page
▸▸ This title tells exactly what someone could expect to find if they viewed the page. Be sure to expand on your title using some similar words, but in more detail.

Key word tag or phrase
▸▸ This tag contains, in order of importance, the key words people would search for when looking for your site and words that are listed in the content text of that particular page. You should have no more than 170 key words in the description phrase and should not repeat identical words/phrases. For example, you could have computer, computer board, and computer system, but computer, computer, computer will get your results kicked out of the system.

NOTE: For additional suggestions, go to www.xplorenet.com and download articles covering the Search Optimization Process.

ATTRACTIVE CONTENT

Search engines look for content. The content of your Web page text is what most search engines look at, but each will have a different take. How do you meet the standards for all the different engines? You don't. You want to prioritize by visitors. Make sure the content is relevant to your targeted user and then let go. If you try to provide different content for each engine you'll lose your key visitors. Here are some brief guidelines:

Establish a clear purpose:
▸▸ Provide the purpose in the main page paragraph describing your company and products and services.

Stay on the subject:
▸▸ Make sure the content fits the subject and the key words—stay on track.

Review for the word weight:
▸▸ Try not to repeat words in the content unless it has specific relevance.

Web visitors:

▸ Keep in mind who visits your site. What content will be important to each visitor and how can you help them complete your chosen "calls to action".

Here are some dos and don'ts of search optimization:

▸ Do learn how to write your Web site using targeted key words and key-word phrases or, utilize the services of a qualified and experienced Web content copy writer.

▸ Don't try to hide text links from the search engines. All content should be created for the user to view.

▸ Do use these key word phrases in your title tags, visible HTML text (head-lines, introductory paragraph, product descriptions, conclusion, and calls to action), Meta tags, alternative text, and anchor text.

▸ Don't utilize a Flash introduction (or splash page). They can hurt your list-ing in many search engines.

▸ Do make sure your site has quality content that visitors will read and spend time researching.

▸ Don't buy a package where they submit your site to millions of search engines. Focus on the top 10 engines.

▸ Do make sure one of the navigation schemes on your Web site is search-engine friendly. This means making sure that your menu and content have text links. They can be embedded text links or a set of links that corre-spond to navigation buttons.

▸ Don't use automated software that generates thousands of pages—stay with specific, quality content.

▸ Do submit your site to the major directories.

Utilizing the correct search engine optimization plan can tremendously enhance the way search engines list your site over others. If your pages are optimized, then you will have a large advantage over your competition.

Email Marketing (4.6)

Purpose: Understand how to implement the proper email tools to match online objectives to business goals

Key Points:	In this section you will learn the proper way to set up and implement email tools, based on your budget restraints and potential options.

Email marketing has grown a great deal in usage over the last four to five years. It's gone from the neat, new tool, to the business must. Every professional utilizes email. Therefore, email marketing continues to be a low cost, effective tool for promoting your services or products and generating and retaining customers. However, the evil "spammers" have caused the application to be untrustworthy and bothersome. How do you accomplish your online objectives while staying away from becoming a spammer? In this section we take a look at the CAN-Spam laws, creating a database of addresses, messaging, email newsletters, and e-nnouncements, helping you build the email strategies of your Web plan.

CAN-SPAM LAWS

Before you get started, you must have a clear understanding of the new spam laws. On December 8, 2003, the United States Congress passed the Controlling the Assault of Non-Solicited Pornography and Marketing Act of 2003 (the "CAN-Spam Act" or "Act"). The CAN-Spam Act defines commercial email as any email message "the primary purpose of which is the commercial advertisement or promotion of a commercial product or service."

The CAN-Spam Act creates a uniform "opt-out" standard, meaning that it prohibits the transmission of unsolicited commercial email unless the recipient has asked the sender to refrain from sending such messages. The Act also creates new criminal penalties for falsifying transmission and routing information in email headers or engaging in other practices designed to conceal the identity of the sender. Email header information that is technically correct nonetheless will be considered false and misleading under the Act if it includes an originating email address that the sender accessed through hacking or fraud. This provision is intended to address situations in which spammers obtain unauthorized access to an innocent party's email account and use it to send spam.

EMAIL STRATEGIES

Now that you understand an overview of the new law, how do you implement a successful plan? One key to setting up your plan is to pick the ones that match your objectives, resources, and budget. According to Doubleclick, a leading provider of email tools, "The better performing companies are making significant efforts to improve list hygiene and data collection processes (as evidenced in reduced bounce rates), as well as conducting better targeting based on mailing segment characteristics and historical response to email." Email promotions must fit the marketing objectives of the company. A successful firm leverages offline campaigns such as price reductions, coupons, sell outs, and other activities with the proper email list and message.

One of the biggest challenges you'll face is learning which online marketing strategies fit your objectives and which ones don't. There is a ton of misinformation about email marketing. It can be very difficult for anyone to figure out what really works. Most people end up attempting outdated concepts or utilizing incorrect tools.

CREATING THE LIST

The first step is to understand the value of an opt-in list. As mentioned in the Can SPAM Law, you must only send to recipients who have opted in to your list. You might have a great offer, but if you send it to the wrong list, it will not be effective. Therefore, you have to start building the list. How do you do this? On the Internet, list buying is complex and confusing when compared to the world of direct mail, where you can examine a standard-format rate card, review demographic data, and get help from an experienced list broker. The email list business has few standards, and it can be hard to be sure with whom you are dealing.

Simply start with your customers and prospects and grow from there. Stay away from the spammers and bulk emailers who will send your message to thousands of people. After you've started creating your database from current customers, vendors, contacts, prospects, etc. find a reliable opt-in email list owner or broker. Make sure you're dealing with a legitimate company, with a good track record. Plan a time to talk on the phone and make sure they have a legitimate business address. Review the method they used to compile the list and make sure recipients opted in. How do they define permission-based? A potential source to start your process is Direct Email List Source, a Web directory of opt-in email lists.

MESSAGING

Now that you understand the list process, how do you formulate the right message? How do you make the right offer to the right user, at the right time? Have a strategy for both HTML and plain text email. A good strategy and quality copywriting can make a big difference when emails are sent out in plain text. Furthermore, for HTML emails, 'creative' becomes your most important element. Creative refers to the design, concept and copy of the email advertisement piece.

The offer must be clear and compelling. This means you must define what you are going to give to the net and what actions you would like them to take once they have that offer. Tell them, step-by-step, what you want them to do. Make sure your offer is compelling by giving the customer something of value with a specified time period to complete the purchase. For example, they can receive two products by buying one or 40 percent off the normal price if purchased by Friday.

We recommend that the copy be brief and straightforward, focus around the offer. Pay close attention to the subject line. Stay way from subject lines that look like spam, like "free", "buy today", etc. Make it simple, and short, while implying a benefit. It must be both interesting and convincing and does not have to involve a financial transaction. You might offer a free gift in exchange for marketing data; perhaps the user can download a free software program in exchange for providing personal information or filling out a survey form. Or you might offer a free newsletter. In this case, the user might not have to give anything in return; it's enough for them to let you send them information every week or monthly. The offer is critical to the success of your email effort. You need to be crystal-clear about what your offer is, and you need to be crystal-clear in communicating it to your recipient.

EMAIL TOOLS

When it comes to email tools and strategies, there are a million choices. In order to have successful campaigns, you will need to understand the marketing objectives and the options like enewsletters, eannouncements, messaging, and delivery, to implement a successful plan.

A key tool for small to medium businesses is the email newsletter. The largest challenge with an email newsletter is the process of opt-in tools. Opt-in is when some one agrees to receive your email. They either sign up via the Web or email, or they may verbally agree to be on your list. The opposite of opt—in is SPAM. A successful email newsletter has great, pertinent content, is nice looking, and offers solutions. In fact, the best ones don't just offer news, but tips and value as well. They help the recipient either make a purchase decision, research the product or service, or give critical information. They have to offer something to the recipient with a properly crafted call to action, not just a bunch of links back to the sender's main page. According to Deb Daufeldt, founder of Second Story Solutions, a leading provider of email newsletters in the rocky mountain region, "Balancing relevancy and timeliness is the key to successful email communications. An experienced marketer more than likely wouldn't send a special on snowshoes to a list of unknown Florida residents during the heat of the summer. Getting the right information to the right recipients at the right time can help to ensure a lucrative marketing campaign." Email newsletters can be a tremendous waste of time and resources if not done properly. If the newsletter is done effectively it can increase sales. The email newsletter offers you the ability to deliver your message to your target audience on a regular basis with a low budget. In fact, newsletters that simply provide information on your latest products and recent company news will only be viewed by your clients or by people who really like you. In order to increase new customers or improve repeat sales, you must provide objective information that helps them personally, or helps their business.

Here are some helpful tips:

▸▸ Make an impact:
Provide a well-designed "look and feel" and an interesting title that catches the recipient's attention

▸▸ Ensure deliverability:
Make sure your enewsletter will reach the reader's email box. Utilize a third-party system like Strongmail (strongmailsystems.com) to work with SPAM filters.

▸▸ Provide value articles:
The stories should enrich the recipient's life, help them solve problems, keep them up to date on industry news, and/or compare their business to specific case studies.

▸▸ Send targeted information:
Understand your subscriber's preferences and only send them information which the have shown interest in.

▸▸ Use a third-party system:
There are so many third-party providers that you don't need to reinvent the wheel. Most of them offer tools to manage multiple campaigns, define subscriber groups, create content, and track conversion rates.

▸▸ Send to your prospects on their schedule:
Ask your recipients when they want to receive the newsletter—daily, weekly, monthly, quarterly, etc.

▸▸ Ask for feedback:
Ask for immediate feedback. Ask recipients to reply to surveys, offer customer experiences, and feedback on which articles offered them the most value and information. Use the feedback to customize your next mailing.

E-ANNOUCEMENTS

An email promotional piece goes hand-in-hand with a newsletter. It should offer the user/customer an opportunity to do business with you. The most common offer is to assist the user to purchase your product. Offers that make sense include "sign-up free", "receive a discount", "buy by a certain date", and "closing out inventory." Promotions should be timed to fit your company's business objectives. Be careful not to send too many, but make them relevant or tied to an event or specific date. This type of email must be brief and to the point. A half page is perfect with one or two graphics and an attention grabbing call to action.

The key to any email strategy is the end result. Most firms utilize an email tool to convert Web site visitors into customers. The following tip and statistic can help your planning:

▶▶ Improve the landing page:
   The landing page is the first page viewed after the user clicks from your newsletter or eannouncement. This page is critical to your success. It must be visually appealing, have the right calls to action, and make sense for the audience.

▶▶ Utilize an email newsletter:
   Enewsletters are alive and well. In fact, according to a recent study by MarketingSherpa, 90 percent of B2C (business to customer/client) and B2B (business to business) marketers are sending out enewsletters

   ○ 60 percent of these companies plan to increase spending on e-newsletters in the coming year.

Email tools and strategies are important whether you're promoting to an internal audience or to the external Web. We've covered several parts of the email section of your Web plan. Your email campaign will fail if all-important areas are not addressed—SPAM overview, address database, messaging, the offer, and the "look and feel".

Affiliate Marketing (4.7)

Purpose:	Understand what an affiliate program is and how to correctly implement it
Key Points:	In this section you will learn what an affiliate marketing process is and the best method for implementing it. We will cover some tips on potential vendors and processes.

Affiliate marketing has been on the Web for a very long time, but now it has begun to make more sense than ever. An affiliate marketing program is defined in a couple of ways. A system of advertising in which site A agrees to feature buttons from site B, and site A gets a commission on any sales generated from site B. It can also be applied to situations in which an advertiser may be looking for marketing information, rather than a cash sale. Also, it is a business relationship with a merchant or other service provider who allows your business to link to that business.

THE PROCESS

When a visitor clicks on the link at your site and subsequently makes a purchase from the merchant, you receive a commission based on the amount of the sale, a referral fee or a pay-per-click fee. These vendors typically sell goods and services or provide appointments or leads to you. You typically link directly to them and pay for either traffic to your site or the actual conversion of a customer. The program is based around password-protected technology that tracks the traffic or conversions. Most programs are set up for large retailers like Wal Mart, Target, or Dell. However, there are medium and small-sized programs that offer a low set-up fee and modest commission plans. You can easily target your established user groups.

Understanding which affiliate marketing program on the Web can help you grow revenue is the starting point. Now, how do you implement a program? Here are some helpful tips:

▸ Establish your target audience.

▸ Set up the budget (what can you afford to pay to receive the customer)?

▸ Research the various opportunities on the Web.

Affiliate marketing is a Web tool that is often overlooked. Most firms are not aware of the benefits of implementation, nor do they know where to find the right program. You should spend some time researching the options and implement the program that fits your needs best.

Strategic Alliances (4.8)

Purpose: Understand how to form strategic alliances and how to make them successful

Key Points: In this section you will learn the proper ways to form strategic alliances on the Web. We will cover what to look for and how to implement the relationship. You'll understand how to maintain the alliances and keep them beneficial for all involved parties.

Every sales book in the world seems to describe the importance of strategic relationships. However, when it comes to the Web, many businesses either overlook strategic alliances or do not understand how to set them up. We touch on a few ideas and review a method to forming the alliances and keeping them strong.

Most businesses have strategic alliances, which are defined as agreements between firms in which each commits resources to achieve a common set of objectives. Firms often form strategic alliances with a wide variety of partners: customers, vendors, competitors, education sources, or government. Through strategic alliances, companies can improve competitive positioning, gain entry to new markets, supplement critical skills, and share the risk or cost of major development projects.

STRATEGIC ALLIANCE ON THE WEB

How do we do this on the Web? The process includes the following:

▸▸ Define your business vision and strategy in order to understand how an alliance fits your objectives

▸▸ Evaluate and select potential partners based on the ability of the firms to work together toward a common goal

▸▸ Develop a working relationship and mutual recognition of opportunities with the prospective alliance

▸▸ Negotiate and implement a basic or formal agreement that includes systems to monitor performance.

Strategic alliances for the Web typically include link exchanges and traffic push. This is where you incorporate a linking strategy to increase traffic to your site, and your results, in the search directories. When you have identified alliances you can exchange Web site or application links, linking users back and forth between the sites. In addition, you can push traffic to each other, specifying service offerings through content, text, graphics, and direct requests to visit the ally's site.

BENEFITS

The benefits of a properly established strategic alliance are immense. These benefits allow you to:

- Reduce costs through economies of scale
- Increase access to new technologies
- Increase knowledge
- Enter new markets
- Beat competitors
- Reduce sales cycles
- Increase traffic
- Improve your bottom-line

Beta Test (4.9)

Purpose:	Understand the process for testing new online promotional ideas
Key Points:	In this section we will cover tips and processes for beta testing your promotional ideas. This includes a testing process and matching the results to the overall sales and marketing objectives.

At this point you've decided which online marketing tools to use. You will need to do some beta testing to make sure your results match your assumptions.

THE PROCESS

Specifically, beta testing your online marketing strategies involves understanding how each test variable will be tracked to the desired result. This means performing test campaigns, keeping result records, and calculating and comparing the results. The tool/idea that worked the best gets your time, energy, and budget. What does this include?

▸▸ Determining which element(s) of an email, banner ad, or search directory tool you need to test. Try to test only one idea at a time.

▸▸ Identify which tools will be tested.

▸▸ Identify each tool with a unique tracking code.

▸▸ Keep quality test results (either use a Web-based tool or an Excel spreadsheet).

➡ Implement the test campaign.

➡ Track and compare results to determine which tool(s) worked the best

➡ Increase the budget on the tools that worked best

  o For example, if you tried the phrase "pets in Colorado" in Google, and it had the best results, implement an additional phrase called "pets in Denver."

Track & Adjust (4.10)

Purpose:	Evaluate different tracking tools and processes and implement the proper changes
Key Points:	In this section you will learn to track your promotional ideas and make the proper adjustments. This includes tools, time frames, and objective data analysis. In the end, you will know when to stop a campaign or heighten the activity.

The choice of Web traffic tracking tools is somewhere in the neighborhood of 500. So how do you pick the one(s) that are right for you? The first basic tool is the software to track the simple traffic on your site. Webtrends owns the market with nearly 90 percent of Web hosting firms offering a Webtrends package. WebTrends offers hits, page views, user sessions, and channels.

TRACKING TOOLS

If you want to know the progress and effectiveness of online marketing campaigns before they are over, then you'll need a method to track the activity on your Web site. There is no shortage of reliable Web metrics services and software available today. Unlike many of the Web metrics tools of the past, today's are more intuitive and user friendly. By learning to use a Web analytics tool, you'll be able to determine what drives customers to your Web site, what they understand, and what drives them away.

Before you start to conduct research on the software vs. ASP (Active Server Pages) and Web analytics tools available, there are several factors to consider:

1. Determine the technical level of expertise for both the person responsible for pulling the correct data, and the person in charge of interpreting the data. Many companies incorrectly assume that a technical person can handle both. Make sure the person is in charge of interpreting the data is taking a marketing approach to what the data may reveal.

2. Real time versus retroactive: ASP models tend to provide information in real-time, while log files take a retroactive approach to examining and making sense of Web traffic. A large e-commerce Web site is an ideal candidate for an ASP-based solution. If your Web site doesn't change much, or you don't drive lots of traffic to your site via online marketing, software (usually a log file analyzer) is probably suitable for your needs.

3. Monthly visitors: do they fluctuate wildly? In general, the more visitors you have, the better off you'll be with an ASP-based solution.

4. What do you want to measure? Seems like an obvious question, but you'd be surprised by the number of people that don't know what they should be tracking. If you're one of them, think about what drives your business (both costs and revenue). You can track at least one of these major elements on your Web site.

Here's a short list of well known Web analytics providers. They usually offer either an ASP- or Software-based solution: Click Tracks, Core Metrics, Omniture, Sane Solutions, Urchin, Webside Story, Webtrends, etc.

MAKING ADJUSTMENTS

As in any marketing campaign, it's essential to establish a baseline from which you'll be able to measure all future activity. Progress always needs a point to start from. One of the most important things you'll need to do to define a baseline, as well as keep track of key metrics and performance of your Web site, is to determine what exactly you'd like to track. Don't let this task overwhelm you. Although the Web offers nearly an unlimited number of combinations of pages that can be viewed, it is only that combination of pages that drive your business that you need to worry about. In other words, identify the pages that have the most impact to your business. Examples are: sign up forms, download information, "have a sales person contact me", shopping carts, customer service/help, etc.

Next, look at the pages that naturally precede those impact pages. You'll want to map out a natural path back to the home page (and if you're using email, banner ads, or search engines, follow that path back to that referring traffic). You've just defined a navigation path that you believe is a typical way for visitors to find you. Now we've identified what we want our visitors to do, and we've determined how they will probably find those critical Web pages. Here are some tips for tracking and making adjustments to your plan:

▸▸ Stick to the plan:
The key to properly utilizing the right online marketing tools is patience. It can take 12 to 18 months for optimized pages to and email databases can take years to build up enough addresses for success.

▸▸ Capture email responses:
Place specific words in the subject line (creating a tracking code). For example, if you have an e-mail announcement or newsletter going to three different groups you would put new product in the subject space going to group 1, product update in the subject space going to group 2, and introducing product "name" in the subject space going to group 3. In addition, use multiple email aliases to track the path (info@, sales@, product1@, Denver@, etc.).

▸▸ Stay consistent:
Similar to any direct mail campaign, online marketing tools must be used and tracked consistently. Set up a tracking schedule.

DEFINE GOALS

Now it's time to define the goals—what you would like your Web site to do. As an example, if you are currently convincing 1 percent of all visitors (i.e. if 100 visit, 1 completes the form) to complete an online ordering form, set a goal of 3 percent over 3 months. The timeframe really depends on you and the sales cycles associated with your business. Make sure you capture all lead generation, online activity, and end results for at least three months. Capturing and analyzing 1-2 months worth of data won't take into account seasonality, or unusually external factors that may impact your Web site. In other words, it's hard to make general assumptions about your Web site based upon one point in time. Three months will allow you to establish a trend and allow you to have a more detailed view of the health of your Web site and its ability to meet visitors and customer's needs.

Using your Web analytics software, you should be able to analyze how visitors use your Web site. Items to consider include:

- Which sequence of pages delivers the best results?

- What pages tend to confuse people (abandonments)?

- What are the key pages visitors view before they take your Web site's call to action?

- If you're paying for online marketing, what referral source provides you with the best quality (defined as those the take the call to action) visitors and Web traffic?

Remember, we're way beyond the number of monthly visitors. We want the number of monthly visitors that take the action we want them to take.

If you're running a campaign, it's critical to examine the relative success of the campaign before it's over. You may decide to use micro-goals at specific intervals as benchmarks. In general, you'll see the most activity from online generated marketing initiatives early after their release (search engines excluded). After about two to three weeks, you may see some residual sales from the campaign, but on average, most of the activity takes place early in the campaign. That's why it's critical to measure success from the get go.

No matter what you've established in your Web plan, make sure you track and make the proper adjustments. Customers, technology, and competitors are constantly changing. If your plan is outdated, then your company may become outdated as well.

COMPLETION OF MODULE 4

Now you've completed the four phases of your Web plan. Refer to Module 5 for the outline and details of a properly constructed Web plan. The drive phrase is important to your organization whether you're promoting the new site or application to an internal audience (employees) or external (customer, partners, and prospects). We attempted to give you an overview of all the options and how to make the best choices. After completing modules 1-4, your new Web project is complete and has the proper strategies to be promoted to the all your target audiences successfully.

MODULE 5: PUTTING IT ALL TOGETHER

5.0 Putting it all together

Congratulations. You finished four of the five modules in this book. At this point you should have a good feel for all the various parts of a Web plan. Now your Web strategies will be defined and well organized. Also, you probably have many more questions than answers at this point. This is good—you're well on your way to succeeding on the new Internet. In the last module, we attempt to tie all the steps together and even provide you with a basic Web plan outline.

According to Forbes 500, most CEOs expect to generate almost 40 percent of their sales through the Internet within the next 10 years. It is more important than ever to have a Web plan. The traditional methods of marketing like television, newspapers, and magazines will continue to shift their attention more to the Internet and away from traditional media. Now is the time to understand how all of your Web strategies fit into a custom Web plan, enabling your firm to grow and succeed in the future.

All Businesses are Ebusinesses (5.1)

Purpose:	Understand the new Internet and what it really means to be an ebusiness
Key Points:	In this section we will tie all the modules together, providing an overview of ebusiness and what successful implementation looks like. We provide a Web plan outline as a finishing step.

According to Google, an ebusiness is defined as commerce conducted in cyberspace. It is the execution of real-time business processes with the assistance of Internet technologies. In essence, its business on the Internet—but it also includes all the processes involved in operating business electronically. The term 'ebusiness' is derived from such terms as 'e-mail' and 'ecommerce,' and includes not only buying and selling, but also servicing customers and collaborating with business partners.

The ebusiness is a buzzword used by many marketers in the new business environment. Many think of the term as selling products on a Web site where a transaction takes place. The reality is that every business is now an ebusiness.

Every company, organization, school, etc. does some type of business on the Web. If you are not thinking of your business as an ebusiness, you're probably falling behind. Customers expect you to do business on the Web and do it well. This ranges from providing simple contact tools to online account management. Today's business environment is not just about sales, marketing, product development, etc, but performing all the requirements of ebusiness. If you have not started to research and understand the true opportunities of ebusiness, you'd better get moving.

Successful Implementation (5.2)

Purpose:	Understand what it is to successfully implement the right Web strategies
Key Points:	In this section we provide an overview of what a successful implementation looks like and the potential results that can be expected from it.

As we mentioned in Module 1, if you've successfully implemented a new Web project, then consider yourself lucky. For the most part, new Web projects miss the target and end up being a waste of both money and time. Successful implementation is about creating and following a well-developed Web Plan.

As you go through your next project, observe the areas where the Web plan keeps you and your team on track and helps you hit your objectives. Furthermore, think of the feeling of relaxation and pride you'll have when the projects are completed and your firm grows and succeeds because of the plan.

Successfully building a Web project is about putting all the pieces together at all the right times. Indeed, just as one would implement a business plan, tactics change, competitive environments change, and new opportunities present themselves. The Web plan is simply your road map to success and is not set in concrete. We suggest that you perform analysis and updates on a regular basis (every three to six months is appropriate). With the plan as your tool, the road will be filled with fewer potholes.

Developing Your Staff (5.3)

Purpose:	Understand how to effectively use your internal staff either by themselves or in relation to an outsourced vendor
Key Points:	This section covers the process of improving the communication and skill level of your internal staff to complete your next Web project on time and within budget.

During the past few years we have been asked more and more to assist with developing and implementing a plan for an internal Web team. This includes helping define job responsibilities, skill sets, improving skill levels, and formulating future Web plans. In fact, over the last few years the trend of taking Web development in-house has grown tremendously. The reasons for this trend include more skilled workers, reduced wages, and the importance of the Web in day-to-day business operations. When and how do you develop an internal staff?

KEY FACTORS

Knowing when to expand your internal staff and how to do it are difficult questions. You must take into consideration many factors including budget allowances, resources, and business objectives. You need to consider how the different skills sets of your internal staff will be utilized. If you do not have the right personnel, your projects may not get completed correctly or in a timely manor. On the other hand, if your personnel are under-utilized, the firm will lose productivity because people are sitting idle.

You will need to evaluate how important the Web applications are to your business objectives. Does it make economic sense to outsource them? Or, should you build a large staff that helps increase revenue and profit via online tools? The answers are easily found once you detail the financial implications and the specific objectives in your plan. Many firms understand the economic benefits of proper staffing numbers, utilizing an outsourced vendor only when the need occurs. If you run the numbers and it makes sense to expand your internal staff, how do you do it in the most efficient manner?

METHODOLOGY

Now that you've decided to expand your Web team you must pay close attention to your methodology. First, evaluate the type of work/projects to be completed. Does it require personnel with front-end skills (graphic design, basic HTML, etc.) or do you need staff that understand databases and complex, third party integration (java, .NNET, ASP, JSP, proprietary software, etc.). It is very difficult to find personnel with both skill sets. In fact, the cost of having a person with all of these skill sets on your team may ultimately be cost prohibitive.

MISSING SKILL SETS

Once you've decided which type of personnel your objectives require, determine which skills are missing. By using this approach you can have an outsourced vendor "on call" for projects that come up infrequently. Identify the missing skills and connect them to the specific projects. For example, if you will build a customer service tool in the third quarter, create a list of deliverables and skills required. Let your outsourced partner know when and what the project will be ahead of time.

If you've chosen to use personnel with front-end skills, make sure they receive basic training on back-end applications and programming. They'll need to have some knowledge of the more complex functionality in order to work well with your outsourced vendor. They can also help with front-end recommendations based on their minimal knowledge of what is happening "behind the scenes" or in the code. In addition, if you've chosen personnel with programming or back-end skills, make sure they receive some front-end training. They should understand Photoshop files and usability issues. A little bit of training goes a long way when it comes to personnel who understand the complex issues.

Developing your internal staff is a key component of your Web plan. In the end, you'll need to understand when to add staff, what their job descriptions are, and how their skills help meet all the strategies of your Web plan.

Web Plan Outline (5.4)

At this point you've chosen the firm you're going to work with or identified your key internal players. In addition, you reviewed the first four modules and covered the first part of Module 5. Now you've reached the Web Plan. In the remaining pages of Module 5, we provide an outline for you to design and implement your unique plan. The plan is divided up into sections and provides a step-by-step process for your next project.

If you have an existing plan, this is your chance to make improvements. If you have no plan, time is running out on developing a successful Web strategy.

Get started today.

The plan consists of four main areas—Analysis, Blue Print, Construct, Drive

Visit www.xplorenet.com or call 303.573.1118 x214 for more helpful ideas

WEB PLAN OUTLINE

SECTION 1: ANALYSIS: Strategy Formulation

1. Name of project and strategy meetings—
   PROJECT NAME:
   STRATEGY MEETING NAME:

2. Main purpose or project mission:
   ▸ Define project goals—Write down key goals
      ▪ Goal 1:
      ▪ Goal 2:
      ▪ Goal 3:
   ▸ Identify key business goals
      ▪ Sales =
      ▪ Revenue =
      ▪ Profit =
      ▪ Other business objectives (brand awareness, client retention, etc.) =

3. Key questions to get the analysis portion kicked off. These questions are intended to get your ideas flowing. You will have answers for some of them

now, but many will be answered later on. You'll need to start thinking about them during the Analysis Phase.

- ▸ What does your business success look like a year from now?
- ▸ How will you make your Web pages load quickly?
- ▸ How will you build your credibility?
- ▸ How will you automate portions of your business?
- ▸ How will you achieve SEO (search engine optimization)?
- ▸ How will you collect your customers' information and store it within a database?
- ▸ What are the written metrics?
- ▸ How will you manage the content?
- ▸ How will the Web team you're working with define success?
- ▸ What types of tools will you use to keep ongoing track of revenue increases?
- ▸ How do you plan to keep track of the traffic to the site?
- ▸ How will you collect your customers' information and store it within a database?
- ▸ What types of marketing tools will you use?
- ▸ How will you match traditional marketing channels to the site?

4. Profile the user(s) (define the target audience)
   - ▸ Identify key business goals
     - ■ Target Audience 1:
       - ○ Overviews
       - ○ Demographics (age, income, gender, etc.)
       - ○ Other important notes—
     - ■ Target Audience 2:
       - ○ Overview
       - ○ Demographics (age, income, gender, etc.)
       - ○ Other important notes—
     - ■ Target Audience 3:
       - ○ Overview

    o   Demographics (age, income, gender, etc.)

    o   Other important notes—

5. Establish metrics

  ▶ Our definition of success:

  ▶ Metrics

     ■ Review existing Web traffic reports for the past three months—total page views, average page views per visitor, new and repeat visitors.

     ■ Areas to analyze:

       o   Review of data integrity, sample dates processed, full analysis run, content click-thru analysis, section review for data flow, user experience analysis, identification of all popular conversion points and metrics, path analysis, data-driven summaries, conversion rate analysis (ROI-driven), exit page summary, number of visits to action summary

       o   What should the numbers be?

       o   Gather recent email campaign results ☑

       o   Review sales reports tied to the Web (for example: new customers, average transactions, online forms submitted, etc.)

       o   Review current customer surveys (if available) ☑

       o   Results

6. Evaluate resources

  ▶ Evaluate the pros and cons of available technology used for the database and administration areas (Microsoft .NET, Active Server Pages, SQL Server, etc.

     ■ Options:

  ▶ Evaluate the skills and abilities of your staff or outsourced vendor

  ▶ What technology will be utilized to establish the metrics (server-based, in-house, outsourced, etc?)

7. Initial design thoughts

   ▶ What types of sites and designs are preferred? Competitive sites? Other options?

      1.

      2.

      3.

   ▶ User Interface—initial ideas

      ■ Describe the use experience—

      ■ Match the user scenarios to the business goals and design

      ■ Colors/theme

      ■ Calls to Action

         ○

         ○

         ○

      ■ Initial Navigation options

         ○ How many menu items?

         ○ Positioning?

         ○ Key areas of the site

            ●

            ●

            ●

         ○ How will the site be navigated?

            ●

   ▶ Initial mock-ups completed (minimum of three)

SECTION 2: BLUEPRINT

1. Scope of work—define the scope of work in as much detail as possible

   ▶ Goals

   ▶ Assumptions

   ▶ Changes/challenges

   ▶ Personnel

▶ Deliverables

  ■

  ■

  ■

  ■

▶ Timelines

  ■

  ■

  ■

▶ Cost

2. Creative Brief

▶ State general project information, goals, and relevant background information for the site redesign. This paragraph should be a statement overview of the project as a whole.

  ■ What are the long-term goals?

▶ Perception/tone/guidelines: how should your target audience to respond to your new online presence?

  ■ What does the target audience think about the firm and the current Web site?

  ■ What do you want them to feel?

  ■ How will this new Web site help hit our goals?

  ■ What adjectives can be used to describe the way the Web site and the company should be perceived by the target audience?

  ■ What are some specific visual goals the site should convey?

▶ Communication strategy: how will we convince the target audience?

  ■ What is the overall message we're trying to communicate to the target audience? (Examples: reliability, cost-effectiveness, secure, top of the industry, etc.)

  ■ How will you communicate the overall message? (Examples: via the copy, directed path from calls to action, special offers on the main page, etc.)

  ■ Identify phases of development

- What the identified success measures established in the strategy session? What tools will be used to measure the success?

▸ Competitive positioning:

- How is your company or Web application different from the competition?
- What specifically, are your competitive advantages?
- What areas of the current site are successful and why?

▸ Targeted message: state a single-minded word or phrase that will appropriately describe the site once it is launched.

3. Technology brief

▸ Internal team technology preferences (ex: Microsoft .NNET with SQL database)

-
-
-

▸ Discuss and analyze all functionality requirements in the new Web project

- Review all functionality issues of the existing site
- Discuss which functionality from the old site to keep, and which you won't need
- Discuss possible new functionality needs
- Discuss which sections can be data-driven and which have administration areas

▸ Review the existing database, its capabilities, limitations, and its role in interacting with the Web site.

- What options are available for the new database?
- How is it accessed from the Web?
- Can we read and write data?
- Can the schema be altered or added to?

▸ Evaluate project technical expertise and develop a plan on how it will be utilized in both the development and ongoing maintenance of the site.

- Review current internal technical skills

1.

2.

3.

- Determine if additional skills can or need to be acquired
- Review maintenance and updating options

4. Content
  - ▶ Inventory all existing content ☑
    - What content do we have (from the existing site or in marketing materials)
      - ○
      - ○
      - ○
    - What content needs be created?
      - ○ Copy
        - Sections (and by whom)
          1.
          2.
          3.
          4.
          5.
      - ○ Pictures/graphics
        - For which sections (what needs to be created and by who)
          1.
          2.
          3.
        - What content will be static (HTML) and what will be dynamic (database-driven)
          1.
          2.
          3.
          4.

- What are the timelines for all the content?
  - ○
  - ○
  - ○

5. Usability Testing
   - ▶ Identify the group of users (5 to 20 should work well)
     - ■
     - ■
     - ■
     - ■
     - ■
     - ■
   - ▶ Send out a three to five question a pre-test questionnaire
     - ■
     - ■
     - ■
     - ■
     - ■
   - ▶ Confirm user and time lines
     - What tasks should be accomplished?
       - ○
       - ○
       - ○
       - ○
     - What are the questions? (10 to 25 questions)
       - ○
       - ○
       - ○
       - ○
       - ○

    ○

    ○

- Set up time to perform testing ☑
- ▸ Decide on the method of testing (email, phone calls, or in person)
- ▸ Place results in a database format or an Excel spreadsheet

SECTION 3: CONSTRUCT

1. Project manager(s)—NAME:
   - ▸ Accountable for what?

2. Web-based project management tool:
   - ▸ Username and password:
   - ▸ Ideas for additions to the tool
     - ■
     - ■
     - ■
   - ▸ Problems with the tool
     - ■
     - ■
     - ■

3. Completion of deliverables
   - ▸
   - ▸
   - ▸
   - ▸

4. Testing tools
   - a. Tool: When:
   - b. Tool: When:
   - c. Tool: When:

5. Launch Date:

  ▶ Changes to schedule:

SECTION 4: DRIVE

1. Online Marketing Strategies:

  ▶ What are they?

  ■

  ■

  ■

  ■

  ▶ Goals:

  ■

  ■

  ■

  ■

2. Online marketing tools:

  ▶ Which tools will be used—search marketing, email, affiliate marketing, etc.?

  ■

  ■

  ■

  ▶ What tracking tools will be used for each tactic?

  ■

  ■

  ■

  ■

  ▶ What is the timeline on implementation?

  ■

  ■

3. Ecommerce tools
    ▸   Shopping Cart options

        ■

        ■

        ■

    ▸   Merchant account set up ☑

    ▸   SSL certificate taken care of ☑

    ▸   Products identified ☑

    ▸   Traffic reports set up properly for tracking

4. Online Sales Strategy
    ▸   What online sales tools will be utilized (you may have defined these in the strategy section)

        ■

        ■

        ■

    ▸   Which tools have been built and what will be included in future plans?

        ■

        ■

        ■

    ▸   Which staff members will be involved in the online sales process?

5. Search Marketing
    ▸   Identify 5 to 10 key pages of the site for optimization

        ■

        ■

        ■

        ■

        ■

    ▸   Which Search engines we'll be utilized?

        ■

        ■

- ■
- ■
- ▸ Key words for each page (20 key words is the goal)
  - ■ Page 1:
    - ○
  - ■ Page 2
    - ○
  - ■ Page 3
    - ○
- ▸ Keyword phrase for each page (less than 170 characters)
  - ■
- ▸ Pay-per-click program
  - ■ Select the vendor(s) [most popular are Google and Overture)
    - ○
    - ○
  - ■ Select key words and phrases to use
    - ○
    - ○
    - ○
    - ○
  - ■ Who will monitor the campaigns?
    - ○ In house—☐   outsourced ☐
    - ○
  - ■ What budget range per 30 days?
    - ○ Yearly Budget =
    - ○ Monthly Budget =

6. Email marketing
  - ▸ Email newsletter or enewsletter
    - ■ What system will be used?
    - ■ Is there an existing database of names? (need to be scrubbed)

- ■ Copy?
- ■ Design
- ■ Formats—HTML, plain text, and AOL

7. Affiliate marketing
   - ▶
   - ▶

8. Strategic alliances
   - ▶
   - ▶
   - ▶

9. Beta testing strategies
   - ▶
   - ▶
   - ▶
   - ▶

10. Tracking Procedures
    - ▶ Tracking
      - ■ Report Generation and Scheduled Changes (monthly, first 6 months)
        - o Monthly Reviews
          - • Traffic patterns & Trend reviews
          - • Conversion Analysis
        - o Client Review
          - • Reports delivered
          - • Reviews and recommendations delivered
          - • Changes proposed
        - o Working with Development company to
          - • Incorporate Changes

- A/B testing (if recommended)
- Campaign planning (if recommended)
- Set up Web Analytics Solution
  - Creation of page tagging project plan
  - Profile testing and creation
  - Template edits and timeline for delivery set
  - Initial Data processing check

Visit www.xplorenet.com or call 303.573.1118 x214 for more helpful ideas

ABOUT THE AUTHORS

Bill Young has assisted hundreds of firms since 1996 with the development and implementation of successful Web strategies.

The modules in this book came about through Young's experience, as Chairman and Co-founder of XploreNet, and through trial and error. XploreNet is a leading provider of technology and marketing integration services in the Rocky Mountain Region, serving customers like American Water Works Association Research Foundation, PakMail, and GE.

 www.xplorenet.com

After graduating from Colorado State University with a Bachelors degree in Business Management, Young co-founded XploreNet in 1997 with $700, a few credit cards, and a dream. Young's vision was to build a technology and consulting company that brings a human perspective to a very technology-driven industry.

Young was honored by the Denver Business Journal as a winner of the "Forty Under 40" award in 2000. In addition, he co-authored the book, <u>Brick and Mortar, Click and Order—The Encyclopedia of Retail and Ecommerce</u>™, teaming with Keven Bernard (1995 Retailer of the Year). Their idea was to bring the worlds of traditional retailing and e-commerce together in a dynamic hybrid approach to business.

Co-Author Michael Sevilla is founder of Gravity Metrics (which was purchased by XploreNet in 2004).

Sevilla serves as VP of XploreNet and under his direction, Gravity Metrics was launched with the sole purpose of demonstrating methods to increase sales and achieve the best possible results from a Web project and all online marketing initiatives. Many of GM's past clients come from the advertising, e-commerce, hospitality/resort, and online training industries.

Michael has an extensive background in marketing, brand management, and product management/development for the consumer goods and technology industries, and received an MBA for International Marketing and Finance from Thunderbird.

Visit <u>www.xplorenet.com</u> or call 303.573.1118 x214 for more helpful ideas

0-595-34575-1